TAMING
THE
CULTURE
TIGER

TAMING
THE
CULTURE
TIGER

THE ART AND SCIENCE OF
TRANSFORMING ORGANIZATIONS AND
ACCELERATING INNOVATION

DR. KATE PRICE

LIONCREST
PUBLISHING

TAMING THE CULTURE TIGER

The Art and Science of Transforming Organizations and Accelerating Innovation

ISBN		
	978-1-5445-3451-0	Hardcover
	978-1-5445-3452-7	Paperback
	978-1-5445-3453-4	Ebook

To my clients, who inspire me every day.

Contents

FOREWORD   1

INTRODUCTION   5

PART ONE

CULTURE AND THE CHALLENGES
OF TRANSFORMATION

1   What Is Culture, and Why Should You Care?   15

2   We All Resist Change   33

3   The Power of Social Groups   49

4   How Our Brains and Beliefs Limit Change   63

PART TWO

EXPECTATIONS AND THE ELEMENTS
OF SUCCESSFUL INNOVATION CULTURES

5   What to Expect on the Journey Ahead   81

6   A Unique Adventure   95

7   Envisioning a New Environment   107

PART THREE

PREPARING FOR CULTURAL CHANGE

8   Becoming a Trusted Leader—It Starts with You   133

9   Building a Leadership Team   157

10 Setting the Scene for Engagement   183

11 Understanding the Current State   199

12 A Scientific Experiment   213

13 Conclusion   223

ACKNOWLEDGMENTS   229

REFERENCES   233

Foreword

Industry researchers and consultants have declared that most efforts to fundamentally change the trajectory of an organization fail. More than three decades of working in and leading large life science corporations brings me to support that contention. This is a vexing condition plaguing the corporate world and most certainly the life science industry. There is no shortage of observations for why this is true or proposed tactics to remedy the issue. It's frustrating to witness how progress for the products and services that could benefit the world are missed or delayed due to companies' failed efforts to realize their visions for change. This book brings a much-needed perspective and approach to equip leaders to overcome the failure modes that seem all too common.

It has been my pleasure and privilege to know and work with Dr. Kate Price for the better part of five years. Early on, I learned that Kate was quite different from many consultants one encounters in the corporate world when pursuing change initiatives. As a professional psychologist, Kate was focused on culture in a unique but practical way. She holds the view that to transform a company, you need to transform the culture, and to transform the culture, you need to transform the people—and transform them in a way that does not create resistance, leading to failed attempts to change.

Many organizations operate assuming the leaders have the skills, vision, and direction-setting ability to drive a transformation. However, as I discovered through Kate's coaching, I had to learn and change things about myself and my ways of leading in parallel with driving organizational change. The aha moment for me came when I made explicit in my own mind the notion that for an organization to transform, the leader must transform as well.

This person-centered approach requires specific knowledge, insights, and tools that relate to how people think and feel, beyond where they sit and what they do each day. This is where Kate's approach, chronicled in the book you are about to read, is unique. Kate describes an approach for doing the careful work of considering the complexity of emotions and thinking that reside in the heads of leaders, teams, and individuals, and she outlines how this applies to cultural change and the hurdles you might face.

While these concepts apply to any organization, herein Kate demonstrates, through the use of anecdotes and stories inspired and adapted from her work, a more specialized application for organizations that require highly educated, highly technical leaders and employees—routinely found in the life sciences.

These highly motivated and intelligent scientists and engineers are often used to being the "smartest person in the room" and are deeply motivated to make a difference by designing solutions that improve lives and health and create change in the world. Life science innovation usually requires long lead times and faces a high likelihood of failure. When these features combine, the resulting organizational dynamics are anything but ordinary, underscoring the need for cultures that support innovation and the approach to developing them, which this book offers.

Kate is an insightful scientist in her own right, and she has practiced in complex and challenging environments. This has allowed her to grow and refine her theory and application, and the result of that journey is codified here. Kate is simultaneously a tremendous executive coach and cultural consultant. I have benefited from her challenges, encouragement, and guidance in my own development and transformation, and I am honored to introduce you to this work and to her, both of which I believe can help you become a more successful leader and person.

Aaron Schacht

CEO, BiomEdit

Formerly Executive Vice President for Innovation, Regulatory and Business Development at Elanco Animal Health

Introduction

Have you ever wondered how you can augment innovation in your organization, moving beyond business strategy and process improvement initiatives?

Are you curious about what role culture might play and if it is truly relevant to the day-to-day success of your organization?

Have you speculated if and how as a leader you could create and lead the transformations required for exponential success?

These are questions I commonly hear from executives and CEOs who are thinking about cultural change. And my answer is that if you create an environment in which your people can thrive, then you will elicit their peak performance, and the sky is the limit for your organization. In innovation environments where talent is a prerequisite, it is *culture* that differentiates your level of success.

Most leaders recognize the impact of culture on their organizations, but they don't know how to lead that change. Not only is change uncomfortable, but it also comes with real dangers. This is especially true in corporate environments, where failure leads to blame and blame landing on senior leaders can result in their dismissal.

For scientists leading life science organizations, the conundrum is often far more pronounced. After a lifetime of excelling technically and academically, you are probably accustomed to being right and may cling to the life raft that your knowledge provides. Failure does not feel like an option. It is easier to stay within the comfort zone of your own expertise, sticking to the science and the business processes and strategies that have helped you rise to the top and have, so far, kept you there. It will be uncomfortable to break out of familiar patterns, to explore uncharted territory without your knowledge to guide you. It may feel terrifying, especially if those around you do not understand where you are going and question your decisions.

As a clinical psychologist, I have worked with people from every walk of life, in corporations across industries, healthcare, prisons, and research enterprises. I have lived as part of a tribal community in the remote north of Fiji, and perhaps most significantly, I was an avid watcher of the original series of *Big Brother*! Across all these experiences I found myself asking:

"What enables humans to live together in harmony, work together effectively, and innovate for the success of our species? Why do organizations unwittingly design systems that undermine the very things that would enable this success?"

And again and again in organizations I come across these questions from senior leaders:

"Why should we focus on the so-called soft skills and culture? What do people matter compared to the processes and strategies that are in place to facilitate business achievement?"

Although these questions are valid, experience has taught me that it is *people* who truly drive businesses. Profits, productivity, and efficiency are all worthy goals, but businesses need people to achieve these, and people cannot put forth their best efforts unless they feel integral to achieving those goals.

Successful companies stay successful by building over the long term. They develop positive corporate cultures where leaders and employees are cultivated, retained, and committed to the company and its values. There is a clear vision that everyone is working toward but that allows for adaptation as the landscape shifts. This sense of continuity creates space for uncertainty to exist without stress because employees have confidence that the organization can overcome any challenge. Developing this type of organizational culture over the long term allows for agility and resilience to be incorporated into every facet of the business and enhances every investment and decision the organization makes.

Business goals and strategic timelines are essential, but without a healthy culture, you will fail to discover what your organization could achieve if everyone were on board and pulling in the same direction. There's no denying this journey will require patience and vulnerability. It will take risk and involve uncertainty. But make no mistake: *people* are what will make your organization succeed. Put them first, and never underestimate the power of improving their experience of the workplace.

Why Leaders Matter

With a background as a clinician, scientist, researcher, and consultant, my expertise is in creating cultures where innovation can thrive. Through the processes of Corporate Synthesis, I partner with my clients to build cultures in which people develop the capacity for change, growth, and resiliency, freed from the neurological constraints of fear and uncertainty. This is what I hope to share with you in this book.

Cultural change relies on leaders who are willing to learn and take on the challenge of transforming not only the culture but also themselves, their teams, and each person within their organization.

Ultimately, this approach can lead people to become more flexible and adaptable to circumstances. It enables them to consider multiple perspectives, which is precisely what we need to succeed in life as individuals, as scientists, and as teams. If your organization hopes to keep up with the fast pace of the modern world, remain relevant, and become innovative with its solutions and ideas, then these are the attributes that you need to encourage in all your employees. It is your responsibility as a leader to provide an environment where this is possible.

This book is about you and the people you lead. As a leader of an organization within the life sciences industry, you can have a huge impact on the world if you let yourself. When leading an organization, the way you think, behave, and manage others impacts more than just you and your career; it also affects your team and everyone who works for and around you. You contribute to and shape the environment in which others exist each day. You are a major force on whether it is a good experience where they can share their whole selves, speak up, and operate in ways that are conducive to their well-being or whether their environment is toxic, disengaging, and a drain on their energy and enthusiasm for life.

> **You can have a huge impact on the world if you let yourself.**

Beyond work, you also impact their families because these people—your colleagues—go home at the end of the day. Their moods, well-being, and energy impact their families, their relationships, and the ways in which they go out into the world. You have a significant influence.

The ripple effects of your choices and behaviors create waves in so many ways. Your organization develops new and innovative products that impact the world—whether in health, food security, animal welfare, or another branch of science. The discoveries your scientists make influence the world in positive ways. If you lead them to success, the effect can be huge. But ask yourself, *If I do not encourage them, if I do not create the right environment for innovation and success, who loses? Who will not receive the medication or food they need to survive? Whose welfare suffers as a result of decreased innovation in my organization?*

Your impact on the world is as big as you enable it to be. So if you think developing yourself as a leader is just for yourself and your career, that it is a waste of time to invest in culture, or that it's just too uncomfortable to be vulnerable and authentic and to learn the skills you need to become a leader who inspires others, the better question to ask yourself is:

What is the impact if I do not do this?

Inside These Pages

This book is for life science leaders who are ready to harness the power of the workplace experience to optimize business results. It is divided into three parts designed to help you in the following ways.

Part One builds knowledge by examining what organizational culture is, why it presents such challenges, and explores the complexities humans present for achieving transformation.

With this knowledge in place as a basis of understanding, in Part Two, we explore why every change process should be unique. Your organization's path to change will not be the same as anyone else's, so a simple cultural change model will not work, but there are underlying elements of successful innovation cultures to consider as you develop your vision.

After framing the complexities involved, in Part Three, we look at why it is necessary to become a leader who can inspire change in others before embarking on transformation efforts, the necessary prerequisites to beginning cultural change, and how to approach them. This part is hard, and most leaders don't like that. It is much easier to maintain the status quo, relying on practices and processes that are well established, or to skip ahead, perhaps by bringing in a consultancy who can do all that uncomfortable "people stuff" for you, thus providing a convenient avenue for blame when the strategy does not work out as planned.

However, if you can take the road less traveled and become a leader who dares, then you will be able to take on the next stages of transformation by building a team that can lead together, in alignment, to drive the organization's ambitions. Together, that team will move forward to engage and inspire the rest of the organization to embrace, rather than resist, cultural change and enable the creation of a culture that serves every individual, alongside the financial and business goals of the organization. This can become the legacy of your leadership—beyond the tangible results of product development and process improvement, you'll leave behind a culture that can sustain both itself and future innovation.

Although the principles of leadership and cultural change presented here are applicable to many organizations, this book is tailored specifically for leaders in the life sciences industry where I often find myself working. My belief is that scientists have a unique mindset that, if applied to cultural change and human processes, can tap into great rewards and faster transformation.

Throughout this book, I draw on examples from my experiences with the people, leaders, and organizations with whom I have worked. To protect the confidentiality of my clients, I have created the fictional organization of BioPharmaTech (BPT) and characters who exist within it, all of whom are amalgamations of my real-life clients and organizations that shared similar experiences.

If you want to know whether this book will answer every question concerning cultural change, the answer is almost certainly not. There is no one answer for any organization. Instead, my intention is to provoke new ways of thinking and introduce you to many concepts that are relevant to cultural change and the reasons that humans resist them. I aim to increase your awareness and your understanding of the dynamics within your organization. However, I cannot tell you how to change yourself or your organization's culture. The responsibility for change does not come from the author or facilitator; it must come from the individual or organization. Change is your responsibility—or, in the case of an organization, the responsibility of each person within it. This is not something that someone can do for you.

Culture is driven by people, and people are messy and complicated. To transform it, you have to embrace the complexity, ambiguity, and uncertainty of taming the culture tiger. It is not up to someone else to take on the task; it is up to leaders like you. This book will empower you to learn, to change, and to grow—but only if you commit to taking action.

If that sounds like you, then let's begin.

PART ONE

CULTURE AND THE CHALLENGES OF TRANSFORMATION

1 | What Is Culture, and Why Should You Care?

The role of culture is that it's the form through which we as a society reflect on who we are, where we've been, and where we hope to be.

—WENDELL PIERCE

Lindsay, Chief Executive of Global Innovation and Development at Bio-PharmaTech (BPT), wanted to transform the culture of her research and development (R&D) organization. She recognized that although the organization was filled with amazing scientists who were smart, skilled, and experienced, they were not achieving at levels that she had anticipated. Clearly, something else was going on. She understood culture to be a critical component in success, and she wondered if it was the missing element for her organization.

As we talked, it became clear that she did not fully understand what culture encompassed or how to gauge what was happening within her company. With no clear starting point, Lindsay was at a loss for where to begin and reliant on simplistic ideas and models for change, which to date, had brought about the opposite of her desired results.

Unfortunately, Lindsay's story is common in the corporate world.

What Is Culture?

Culture can be nebulous and poorly understood. Even among those who study it, there is debate between fields about how to define it. I have heard it described as being like air quality: hard to see, but you know how it feels to breathe in.[1] You can determine whether there is a fresh, regenerative feeling that energizes you or a sense of toxicity from which you want to protect yourself. The ever-popular iceberg metaphor fits well too.[2] Much of culture is formed by assumptions, beliefs, and behaviors that are hidden beneath the surface and are not readily available for examination or change. Perhaps unsurprisingly, as a clinical psychologist, I see culture as the personality of a company. It's the "more or less consistent pattern of thought and actions" that exist within a group.[3]

We often talk about personality in our day-to-day lives. We reflect on how we got aspects of our personalities from our parents or whether we like a colleague's personality. But if asked to describe the meaning of personality, most people would be unsure. As a psychologist, I define it as the traits and patterns existing over time that influence the consistent thoughts, feelings, and actions taken by an individual.[4] We tend to see personality as stable and unchanging. We assume that a difficult coworker can't change because "it's his personality," or, in the case of a family member, that "it's just the way he is; he's been like that since he was a child." The truth is more complex.

Personality can change. It is adaptable, but it takes time. Our beliefs, habits, and emotional responses are deeply ingrained in the neural structures of our brain. These are real, physical pathways that have grown and developed into complex networks over our lifetimes. Like an often-trodden path in the grass, they are carved deeply over time, eventually becoming paved highways that shuttle us quickly to our destination or our habitual responses. Changing these pathways once established takes considerably more time and effort than it did when our personality was first beginning to form. It can be done, but it requires motivation, intention, and time.

Culture is similarly embedded within an organization and in individuals' neurology but is also malleable with intention. It is comprised of the underlying beliefs, assumptions, values, and behaviors of individuals and is guided by the way they perceive the expectations of the environment within which they operate. Like someone's personality, an organization's culture is unique. Since your organization's culture is different from anyone else's, your methods of change will also need to be customized to your circumstances.

Culture is constructed from the minutiae of everyday life. It is the accumulation of individual actions, attitudes, and beliefs that shape community opinion and, in turn, future thinking and behavior. The norms of behavior, thinking, and emotional intelligence, as well as routines and traditions, influence what is created. Culture is shaped by what we say and do and how we perceive, interpret, and respond to others and our environment, not by lofty goals and corporate vision statements.

Two Sets of Rules: The Written and the Unwritten

I have found that in many organizations, there are two sets of rules. The first set is on websites and walls, listed in your handbook, and promoted in the organization as a set of values to live and work by. The second set is the one that matters. It is the one that you encounter when you speak out or that you hear whispered by watercoolers.

Lindsay's organization was no different. BPT was an organization with a clear purpose: to improve lives and empower people to take care of their health by delivering innovative and affordable solutions to healthcare challenges around the globe.

Their cultural ideals placed openness, collaboration, innovation, and striving for excellence front and center. But what is promoted as a vision rarely reflects what is actually happening. As we looked deeper at BPT, we found employees were unwilling to take risks, identify problems early, or own mistakes due to a fear of blame and repercussions from management. Negative perceptions spread quickly, and discontent was soaring. Performance-related pay was based on meeting deadlines, and this pressure created anxiety and a tendency to cut corners. We also heard positive stories about collaboration and close-knit teams, as well as the enjoyment people felt from the scope of the work itself. However, the negatives were detrimental. The science was suffering and innovation was declining, yet no one spoke openly about these problems.

These are the real rules that set the personality of your workplace and determine how your organization functions. When people see or feel a distinction between the written and unwritten, the unwritten rules win the day. To make a change, this is what you must address.

Culture is in the details—in the small, everyday facets of the work, how people experience it, and what they really think and do. Because culture is a nebulous concept, it can seem elusive at times. However, it is a living, breathing part of your organization. It fluctuates daily and can take on a life of its own and develop in unforeseen directions.

Remember, your organization will have a culture whether it happens arbitrarily or you build it mindfully. The strongest leaders intentionally create cultures that move their organizations into the future.

Why Does Culture Matter?

As organizational processes become increasingly automated, the demands of human labor are changing. Cognitive, social, emotional, and relational skills are rising to the forefront of companies' needs as the push for creativity, communication, and innovation becomes increasingly important.[5] Culture is critical to the development of these factors.

Most of the leaders with whom I speak know that culture is important, and Lindsay was no exception. She'd read how companies with strong cultures can see a fourfold increase in revenue growth.[6] She recognized that companies that consistently appeared in the Fortune Best 100 Companies to Work For list were realizing cumulative returns of up to 495 percent, compared to 156 percent on the S&P 500 and 170 percent on the Russel 3000.[7] Although Lindsay cared deeply about people in her organization, revenue and profits often spoke louder because she was responsible to a board of directors and shareholders who were less intimately connected with the organization and who demanded results. But knowing that highly engaged workplaces averaged a 10 percent increase in customer ratings and a 20 percent increase in sales, she could connect the worlds of business and finance with people and their experience of the workplace.[8]

Attracting Talent

As we began to think about the human aspects of corporate life and what makes companies successful, Lindsay recognized that the reputation and brand of the organization was critical to her ability to recruit talent. Research showing that 50–84 percent of people refused to join a company with a bad reputation resonated with her. Her HR leader, Sarah, along with 80 percent of recruiters, acknowledged that branding and reputation are a significant factor in acquiring the great talent they need to succeed as a scientific organization.[9] Despite this awareness, little attention was being paid to the myriad of ways that this might play out at BPT.

Culture heavily influences the reputation and perception of an organization's brand. The employee stories of harassment and toxic management at Uber in recent years demonstrate clearly how culture affects reputation.[10] This negativity is difficult to erase from public perception and impacts both hiring and customer relationships, as well as the bottom line. In the modern world, the stories employees tell of their workplace experience are widely available on websites such as Glassdoor and Indeed, as well as through social media and traditional branding. This goes both ways: the COVID-19 pandemic resulted in a 30 percent increase in consumers' positive views of pharmaceutical companies' reputations.[11]

Culture heavily influences the reputation and perception of an organization's brand.

However, this goes beyond successful vaccine development to what Dave Ricks at Eli Lilly called, "a once-in-a-generation opportunity to reset" the industry's reputation. With more and more pharmaceutical companies joining the social and cultural dialogue to sustain their corporate brands, it is clear they believe positive tales of culture also spread and influence perception. The online shoe retailer Zappos mastered this dynamic early by celebrating the stories that brought their values to life and giving equal attention to employee and customer experience. The result: positive media and great employee reviews.[12]

Retention, Job Satisfaction, and Engagement

Friedrich, a senior director reporting to Lindsay, was happy in his role and loved BPT. Still, like 92 percent of US employees,[13] he considered a new opportunity when he was offered a role at another organization with a great corporate reputation. For Lindsay and Sarah, this situation underscored the issue of retention in their quest to create a successful business. The world has moved on from the days of one job for life. The workforce is now transient, and rather than resting on your laurels, you must be active in retaining those whom you have worked hard to recruit.

Culture plays a massive role in retention. Fifty-eight percent of resigning employees cited difficulties with their manager and the workplace culture. This turnover has cost US employers alone more than $223 billion over the last five years.[14] The turnover "themes" that are trending upward are intrinsically linked to culture, including environment, work-life balance, and career development.[15] This is increasingly evident in the wake of the pandemic and the aptly named "great resignation." With the conservative cost of turnover being $15,000 per employee in the United States, total turnover cost in 2016 was $617 billion. Reducing preventable turnover by 20 percent would save over $95 billion a year.[16] The costs for skilled workers and scientists are invariably higher, and the expense is not just in recruitment but also in training, development, and the creation of new team dynamics, all of which generate additional costs because they undermine productivity and performance. With real replacement costs ranging from half to two times a worker's compensation, that could cost a company with just 100 employees $2.6 million a year.[17]

For Bill, an employee at BPT, his work environment, his support systems, and the alignment between mission and values have the greatest impact on his day-to-day satisfaction.[18] These factors are directly related to culture. If you can create a positive experience of these factors, employees are more likely to remain at the organization.

However, satisfaction is not the same as engagement. Since Samilla, a mid-level scientist at BPT, scored high on measures of job satisfaction, the company made assumptions about her engagement and loyalty. However, Samilla occasionally browsed other jobs online. She found herself spending time on family issues at work, and she rarely talked about the positives of her role or BPT. Although satisfied at work, Samilla was not engaged. Even though employee satisfaction reduces turnover, engaged employees are more productive because they go above and beyond the demands of their roles.[19] Therefore, we must go beyond attracting and retaining employees and enable them to engage and perform at their best in the workplace. Of concern for the US economy, Gallup suggests that 63 percent of employees are not engaged at work, with only 13 percent being highly engaged.[20] The

24 percent who are actively disengaged are searching for new jobs, and US employers are spending upward of $2.9 million per day in their search for new workers.[21] This not only costs you in recruitment and retention, but it impacts the perception of your brand, the morale of your current employees, and your business output. Worldwide, approximately 340 million people are actively disengaged with their roles at work, and in the current economy, this is increasing.[22] These statistics also mean that over half of your employees are not performing at their optimum, creating a breeding ground for discontent and negativity, which directly impacts your culture and future success. Engagement and loyalty must be earned, and leaders and organizations must prove themselves deserving of people's time and attention. In this day and age, a paycheck is not enough.

> **Engagement and loyalty must be earned, and leaders and organizations must prove themselves deserving of people's time and attention.**

Happiness and Well-Being

Lindsay told me that many of her peers on the executive team felt happiness was irrelevant in the workplace. I have found this to be a common view in corporate settings where strategy, finance, science, and resources are prioritized. However, if you are one of the leaders who thinks this, take note of the fact that happy employees are 12 percent more productive on average, and unhappy employees are 10 percent less productive than the average.[23] This reduced productivity costs US businesses an estimated $300 billion a year.[24] If you take the time to promote engagement and well-being in your organization, these efforts will translate directly to your bottom line and the success of your organization.

Let's think about Brian's experience. Every Sunday night, Brian dreads going back to work. Although he loves his research into cytokine production and would define himself as extroverted, Brian feels unsafe speaking up on his team. He is concerned about the consequences of doing so, which are felt to be very real throughout his organization. He feels he cannot be himself at work and must always present the right image. His wife is concerned about his mental and physical health.

Brian is not alone in his Sunday night anguish. Approximately 81 percent of employees have similar experiences.[25] The impact on employees' mental and physical health should be a concern for every organization. Unhappiness, disengagement, and stress are often hidden problems, which speak loudly to cultures that do not view these factors as relevant or acceptable. So many executives with whom I speak tell me that stress is not an issue in their organizations. Yet the evidence speaks loudly to contradict this.

With an estimated one million employees per day being absent due to stress in the United States, 80 percent of workers feeling stressed, and many are at risk for burnout—this is an ever-increasing problem in a society that equates busy with productive.[26] Long work hours and high levels of stress are viewed as a badge of honor rather than recognized for their detrimental effect on individuals and organizations. In fact, workplace stress is estimated to cost US organizations around $190 billion a year in healthcare costs alone.[27] The impact is staggering. Since many people will not admit to stress, fearing that it will be seen as a sign of weakness or because they fail to recognize the physical consequences of stress, the real costs are many times higher.

Are you paying attention to your employees' experiences?

For research and discovery organizations, which rely on their employees to be innovative and create new products in a rapidly changing marketplace, the impact is even greater because stress reduces our cognitive capacity. If your workforce is stressed, then you aren't getting them at their best. Their decision-making, creativity, and ability to collaborate are all constrained. Productivity and innovation are reduced, and the very lifeblood of your goals and ambitions to lead your industry are diminished. With this information in hand, ask yourself:

Am I paying attention to my employees' experiences?

Risk and Failure

Top-ten pharmaceuticals spend over $1 million per day on discovering new biological targets and creating new therapeutics,[28] and 75 percent of R&D costs are related to drug development failures.[29] Knowing that about 90 percent of all prospective drugs fail, with costs rising exponentially the further along a product development cycle they go,[30] Lindsay recognized that the ability to fail fast and well is essential to scientific and organizational progress as well as to financial well-being.

Ivana, a biochemist in discovery, realized that the small molecules on which she was working to target RNA had issues. She also knew that the organization had invested heavily in this research and there had been hype due to promising early results. Her team's performance goals for the year were tied to the project's success, and she was reluctant to let down her team and the organization. How would they respond, and what would it mean for her if she were the one who raised the issue? She stayed quiet until another team member identified the same problem and discussed it with her. Together, they raised the problem to management. It was not received well, but action was taken. Between Ivana's observation and that of her colleague, nearly three months elapsed. What was the cost of this hesitancy to the organization?

If your employees are unwilling or unable to speak up about problems or identify mistakes or errors, then there will always be delays. Ineffective products will have their development life cycle prolonged, and the cost to organizations can be massive. Culture can be the differentiator in this instance. How people feel in an organization affects not only their engagement but also their ability to perform, be effective, fail, speak up, and innovate.

Culture profoundly impacts all these issues that influence your business success and much more. It creates the foundation for everything you do. Creating an innovative and forward-thinking culture is a continual balance between thoughtful behaviors that enable people to establish positive environments and the harder, process-driven business elements. Either one without the other will not lead to success. But too often, we focus on one side to the exclusion of the other, seeing them as incompatible rather than two sides of the same coin.

What Is Your Understanding of Culture?

For any project to be deemed successful, it must be delivered on time and on budget. Most attention goes to process and finance, but the greatest risk of failure lies in the human objectives. Unfortunately, little, if any, attention is typically placed here. My own experience of cultural changes in organizations indicates that successful, sustainable change is rarer than in other business change, perhaps because the human factors are of greater significance.

So why are the employees and the impact they have on change so overlooked? It is often easier to deal with the other objectives because we can assign a number or deadline to them. It is not so with the subjectivity of human nature; there are so many confounding variables that it can be overwhelming.

Organizations are prone to oversimplifying concepts to make them easy to implement—perhaps a nice four-step model, for example. When we don't know how to do something effectively, we tend to opt for a process that sounds easy to implement, or we allow someone else to take control. Despite recognizing the importance of culture on business objectives as Lindsay did, only 28 percent of executives say that they understand their organization's culture.[31] If there is a disconnect, leaders don't understand what culture is or how to assess it, let alone how to carry out change in it. How, then, can leaders be expected to drive cultural change that relies on the collaboration and participation of hundreds, potentially thousands, of individuals to be successful?

While leaders are trained in the business and technical aspects of running an organization, it is rare that they get any training on the ways people function within a business environment. Because of this gap in knowledge, they feel impotent in their ability to create change and neglect the human aspects of the organization to the detriment of employees, objectives, and business success.

With a lack of knowledge, many leaders won't take on the responsibility for cultural change. Creating change feels beyond them or outside their role. But if you lead an organization full of people, I would argue that it is a key aspect of your role because most other objectives are accomplished by the people you lead. If you want to create true organizational change, you must apply the same discipline to the human aspects of an initiative as you do to the technical and strategic processes. You need to understand the barriers to adoption that are created in the minds of your employees and work to overcome them. Avoid setting up a situation where employees actively resist change and all your efforts are wasted.

This change in approach will likely require a shift in your own thinking. It will certainly require learning for you and your leaders, as you shift from a focus on strategy and process to fully incorporate the human aspects of business. To create sustainable change, you must bring an understanding of people and culture into your organization at every level because cultural change depends upon the participation of everyone involved.

Culture versus Climate

We must make an important distinction between climate and culture. Very often, I see organizations enter into cultural change processes, only to feel as though they have made significant changes in a short time, perhaps even a few months. This can be the case for companies that work with large consultancies that come in and run a cultural initiative for them. Attitudes swing in the first few months, and people are enthusiastic about the changes. However, this is a change in climate, not culture.

Organizational climate defines how people experience the work environment in the present moment. It relates to the collective experience of everyone in the organization and can be impacted by internal initiatives, such as a focus on employee well-being, or external events, like the economy impacting business or a change in customer preference affecting revenue. Such change is typically short term. It doesn't equate to cultural change because it does not affect the identity of the company or the people within it in any long-term or sustainable way. The organization's personality has not had time to change.

As we discussed, culture is about the organization's identity and personality—the norms, values, beliefs, and assumptions that have developed organically over time and become part of the individual psyche.[32] It can be hidden from plain sight, but it is felt by the people who exist within it.

Climate is much easier to see. It's easier to measure, and unfortunately, this is where most leaders focus their efforts. We see this most visibly in the focus on employee engagement surveys, which primarily indicate climate rather than real behavioral shifts of culture and the underlying assumptions and norms of the organization, and therefore, these metrics shift on a regular basis but do not represent cultural change.

Edgar Schein, a well-known cultural expert, tells us, "A climate can be locally created by what leaders do, what circumstances apply, and what environments afford. A culture can only evolve out of mutual experience and shared learning."[33] It's about the way people experience the workplace and the ways in which they learn, respond, and eventually alter their beliefs, assumptions, and actions at a neurological level. This change takes time.

At BPT, a passive-aggressive culture of blame from the top down led to silence from the ranks. There was an unwillingness to speak out or share ideas. As you can imagine, this culture didn't inspire innovation, and it created serious risks for the business. Consequently, the initial focus of cultural change was the creation of psychological safety. Lindsay and her team engaged in promoting the concept, and over the first year, feedback was great. People were excited by the concepts and engaged with the ideas and initiatives. The employees were confident that the leaders were engaged and actively participating. There were positive changes in engagement, a sense of belonging, and business results. The needle shifted dramatically on engagement scores, with an increase of 14 percent over a three-month period. The organization was thrilled by the change.

But was the culture transformed that year?

No. This was a shift in climate; the cultural transformation was only just beginning. However, this reaction to climate change in organizations is common. It looks so positive. People see and feel the results of their efforts, and they believe that transformation has occurred. They then take their focus off culture, thinking their work is done. Results and surveys show positive results, allowing external consultancies to withdraw with glowing reports. Without the dedicated focus, however, improvements dwindle. Leadership styles revert, sometimes dramatically but usually more subtly. Processes and procedures implemented to support change start to fall apart as people lose the sense of connection between structure and culture. Ultimately, the successful climate change dissipates as you take your focus off it, overwhelmed by the existing culture that has not yet transformed and the subtle messages sent to the organization about your commitment to the process.

Climate is important and will form steps along your path, but do not be fooled into thinking that short-term achievements in behavioral change and climate are equivalent to true cultural change. Sustainable cultural change endures through external pressures, shifts in leadership, and evolving challenges. It requires a long-term approach to alter behaviors and attitudes throughout the organization. These self-sustaining changes rely on changing underlying neural structures within each individual to eventually influence and transform the organization.

If you want to change the culture of an organization, you must understand the ways in which individuals make sense of the world around them, along with their motivations, how they interact with others, and why they may resist or engage with change. This can be difficult to strategize around because the key is in the small details and concepts that we often feel we have little influence on. Culture does not change in the structured ways that new processes and procedures can be implemented. Sustainable change requires a gradual evolution for true transformation to occur in the hearts and minds of the people who make up your organization, and this is what we will explore in the next chapters.

Summary

- Culture is the personality of your organization, formed from the small things people think, say, and do each day.

- Culture is nebulous and hard to define, which keeps people from tackling change, based on their lack of knowledge or experience.

- Leaders rarely have training or experience in understanding people and their motivations.

- Culture has a huge impact on employee engagement, satisfaction, well-being, and productivity. In turn, this affects recruitment, retention, reputation, and the financial health and success of your organization.

- To create successful change in culture, you need to apply the same discipline to the human aspects of your organization that you apply to the technical and strategic aspects.

- Early signs of change are likely to be a shift in climate rather than long-term, sustainable cultural change.

- To change culture and overcome resistance, you must understand how people think, act, and make sense of the world.

- Changing culture takes time. It is a gradual evolution in the hearts and minds of each individual and group within an organization.

FOOD FOR THOUGHT

Simplicity does not precede complexity, but follows it.

—ALAN PERLIS

Solutions should be simple, easy to implement, and sustainable. However, cultural change is complex, and to create practical solutions and implement them effectively, we must first understand the complexity of human nature because humans are at the heart of culture and any transformation you undertake.

In the remainder of Part One, armed with the knowledge of what culture is and why it is so relevant to your organization, we will explore why people think in the ways they do, the reasons they resist change, and what leaders and organizations need to consider during transformation efforts.

The diagram below represents areas that influence the ways we, as humans, think and act. Each is inextricably intertwined with the others. Although for simplicity we can study and speak about each area separately, in reality none exists in isolation.

As you read through the next chapters, I invite you to challenge yourself to identify which areas might be implicated in each aspect we discuss. Invariably, there will be more than one. This is part of the complexity of culture and people and the challenge for leadership. To design a strategy that is truly effective, we must accept that changing hearts and minds is complicated and that a deep understanding of humans will help us overcome many of the difficulties on the journey to transformation.

2

We All Resist Change

If you want to make enemies, try to change something.
—WOODROW WILSON

Your subconscious has you programmed. It knows your comfort zone, and it works hard to keep you where you feel comfortable and safe. It knows that you do not like negative feelings like sadness, rejection, and fear, so it tries its best to help you avoid situations that cause them. If you do something new or try to change, then it will make you feel emotional or physical discomfort. It wants to warn you to stop what you are doing because it does not know what will happen.

Before you begin your journey of cultural change, it is valuable to understand the unconscious mind and why people resist change because these are the major challenges you will face along your path.

In the previous chapter, we focused on defining culture and its relevance to the success of an organization. Now, diving deeper into the mindset of individuals who are essential to the creation of organizational culture, we must acknowledge that there are numerous underlying neurological mechanisms involved in change. We must ask why people fight against change, even when it would benefit them. When we consider proposing change, we must consider how we can win the cooperation and engagement of every stakeholder and overcome resistance.

Let's consider a scenario that Lindsay's IT Director, Ted, recently encountered. The scenario was a simple introduction of a new system, but nothing as complex as a new culture. For several years, employees had been complaining about how the current system did not meet their needs. Ted and his leadership team discussed the issues and investigated options. They found an appropriate tool and contracted with a supplier to set it up. Once installed, the IT department proudly unveiled it to the organization, anticipating widespread appreciation since it solved every problem that had previously been raised. To their surprise, the tool was nearly universally rejected. How could this happen?

Why do people fight against change, even when it would benefit them?

The simple answer is that they presented the tool as a fait accompli—already decided and irreversible. People inherently do not like change that is imposed upon them, and their unconscious reacts reflexively. In the eyes of the employees, this change came out of the blue.

Ted's team had spent eighteen months thinking about the issue, analyzing options, raising questions, and finding solutions. Now they expected the employees to reach the same conclusions after an hourlong presentation! People like to, and need to, be involved when seeking solutions to problems. When change comes as a surprise, it feels imposed because they were excluded from the journey. Their minds have not had time to adapt, question the changes, or analyze how they may be affected. People are initially concerned with what change means for them personally. If you don't address that concern, expect to receive resistance.

We as humans don't hate change in and of itself. We often take adventures, try new activities, or change jobs. We may feel a bit anxious, but we willingly step into the unknown. We do hate change, however, when we have no say. It makes us feel powerless, activating uncertainty and anxiety and triggering our unconscious beliefs and fears. This was true for Laetitia, one of Ted's peers at BPT, when she heard about the new system. It challenged not only her entrenched routines and her methods but also her way of being. She questioned her status as a senior leader who had not been consulted, her self-image, and the ways in which she felt others perceived her. These feelings provoked anxiety, which led her to resist change. Rather than be forced out of her comfort zone, she preferred to stick with her old methods, which undermined Ted's initiative.

It's a common belief that resistance is most prevalent within the rank and file of an organization. However, corporate communication plays a major role in whether resistance occurs. Frequently in my work with organizations, I find that leaders and managers are the ones who resist change, as Laetitia did, because of the challenge to their status, their entrenched ways of being, and their belief in their proven performance methods. The greater an individual's motivation to maintain the status quo when uncertain about what change means for them, the greater their resistance to change will be. And if they don't want the change, they are unlikely to be persuasive in their communications for change as the information cascades through the organization.

Just because you do not see resistance from leaders or people don't speak out directly doesn't mean it isn't there. If people are afraid to speak up about their doubts, those doubts will still undermine your efforts in subtler ways, and corporate communications are likely to be impacted and play a role in change resistance.

So, what is happening in someone's brain when you propose a change?

Tigers in the Mind

Imagine you are walking alone in the woods. Suddenly, a tiger appears in your path. The information arrives at your amygdala, a part of the emotional processing system. Recognizing danger, a signal is sent to your hypothalamus, and thoughts relevant to the situation occur. You become alert and aware of the threat. Your sympathetic nervous system is warned and springs into action. Your adrenals pump out the hormone epinephrine (aka adrenaline). Your heart beats faster to get blood to your muscles. Your eyes widen, and other senses sharpen. Your breathing becomes faster, and small airways open wider to accept more oxygen into your system. Glucose and fats are released from storage sites to provide energy, and your muscles tense as you focus all your attention on the immediate situation. You are primed to respond, to fight or to flee.

I just described an automatic reaction triggered by a sense of threat. The reaction happens so fast that you are not aware of the component parts. The amygdala and hypothalamus are so efficient and well rehearsed that they begin the process even before your visual centers have fully processed the incoming information.[34]

This is the fight-or-flight or stress response.[35]

These instinctive responses improve your chances of survival, enabling you to adapt to situations and respond appropriately to danger. They are triggered automatically when you feel threatened. During the Stone Age, this biological framework was a necessary survival mechanism, and it remains so in life-or-death situations.

However, in the majority of modern environments, fight or flight is not appropriate. Your boss is not a tiger, so fighting or running away will probably not get you a promotion or endear you to the board members. Ted's proposed IT changes were not going to physically hurt anyone, and your deadlines aren't going to kill you (although at times it feels like they might!). Despite this, all of these things that we worry about every day keep our bodies in a stress response. Stress can become so constant for many of us that we feel that it is normal, and we don't even perceive that we are stressed. But the daily stressors that our brains interpret as threats or as beyond our ability to cope[36] keep our hypothalamic-pituitary-adrenal (HPA) axis switched on.[37] This leads to a constant release of chemicals that trigger our pituitary glands to release hormones, which then triggers the release of cortisol from the adrenals. Because our brain continually perceives "threats," our parasympathetic nervous system, which acts as a damper to this system, is prevented from reducing the stress response.

Your boss is not a tiger, so fighting or running away will probably not get you a promotion.

The problem is that as stress redirects your resources to your survival needs, it diverts that energy away from functions that seem a less immediate priority. The result on our physical health is damaged blood vessels from persistent epinephrine surges,[38] weight gain due to physiological changes resulting from elevated cortisol levels,[39] suppression of immune responses,[40] and exacerbation of autoimmune disease.[41]

Processes like digestion, production of growth hormones, and immune functions take a back seat, resulting in further health problems. Our higher-level brain functions also take a back seat when we are in survival mode, and as a result we are less able to perform our work tasks effectively.[42]

Chronic stress increases our vulnerability to mental illness[43] because our emotional resilience decreases.[44] As our physical and mental health declines, we are more prone to stress but less able to cope with it. This pushes us into a negative cycle that impacts our health and our lives but also our ability to work, perform optimally, and contribute to organizational life and success.

Tigers in the Office

Much of my early work and research was based on countering the stress response in populations where extreme and chronic activation led to violent or unpredictable behaviors, mental ill-health, and often incarceration. This work brought me to understand the chronic impact of stress on physical and mental health but also on our ability to perform at work, remain conscious of our own internal states, and be self-aware.[45] Our level of self-awareness impacts our relationships and understanding of others and eventually, in extreme cases, our ability to interact normally with society. With burnout being recognized in 2019 by the World Health Organization as an occupational phenomenon, "resulting from chronic workplace stress that has not been successfully managed," it is vital to acknowledge the amount of stress that we experience daily in modern corporate life.[46]

Work and organizations create a lot of unintentional stress for their employees. Poor managerial relationships, micromanagement, ever-increasing workloads, jobs lost and not replaced that end up doubling workloads, toxic teams, conflict, and not feeling free to speak up about frustrations all produce the stress response. In many corporate environments, people do not feel it is safe or appropriate to share what is going on in their lives outside work, and they may not feel comfortable talking to their colleagues or managers. This kind of stress inevitably impacts how employees function in the workplace. A lack of perceived job control, as Ted's staff experienced, is a known stressor. It increases the risks of coronary heart disease and adversely affects heart health.[47] It also leads to negativity, cynicism, and exhaustion, resulting in disengagement, reduced teamwork, lowered productivity, and higher costs and turnover for organizations.

> **Work and organizations create a lot of unintentional stress for their employees.**

Often, this stress feeds into the culture. If we exist in an atmosphere where speaking up to express that you have too much work is interpreted as failing, then we simply will not do it. No one wants to be judged. No one wants to be seen as complaining, and no one wants to risk their job. The way we are viewed by our managers and colleagues is important to us. It protects our self-esteem and our identity and ensures that we are valued by our team. When we feel these priorities are under threat, our internal subconscious beliefs get triggered, prompting us to take defensive action and, at times, even sabotage our own best intentions.

> For life science organizations that rely on research and innovation for survival, stress is a huge barrier to success.

We say nothing because we do not want to appear weak or difficult. Instead, we trudge on toward burnout and health issues, or we start looking for new jobs. However, if no one knows that we are struggling, then we will not get the practical support we need, and organizations won't acknowledge the depth of the issue. "If no one is complaining about stress, then clearly it is not an issue here!" As a society, we need to acknowledge that everyone experiences stress. It is a normal human response, and the workplace is the leading cause of chronic stress.

Stress is pervasive in our society, in part because we design environments that promote it. Sometimes we see it as a badge of honor or a sign that we are productive. We equate long hours worked with commitment or mistake busy for productive. But stress is none of these things. It is detrimental to our physical and mental health, our well-being, and our productivity. It harms organizations and even our success as a species. It costs our organizations in healthcare, absenteeism, retention, and recruitment because no one wants to work for a stress-inducing organization with no life balance or enjoyment that prioritizes profits over people.[48] Beyond that, for life science organizations that rely on research and innovation for survival, stress is a huge barrier to success.

Our Brain's Capacity for Change and Innovation

It is surprising how much our emotions and anxieties can control our lives. We live in a world where we assume that we are in charge and our minds and bodies are disciplined to act under our direction. I find this is especially true in the scientific community, which often divorces itself from the impact of emotions in search of objectivity. However, when stress takes hold, we are no longer in charge. Our unconscious beliefs have more freedom to interfere as our capacity for logic, reason, and self-regulation declines.

Under prolonged stress, our brains actually shrink, and we lose neurons.[49] Neural networks may be rewired, reducing activity in the prefrontal cortex, which is imperative for our higher cognitive skills, and increasing activity in the primitive parts like the amygdala, which can increase in size.[50] Ironically, this makes us more prone to react to stress, continuing this damaging cycle and accelerating our cognitive decline.[51]

Neurologically, stress blocks our ability to think clearly and make informed choices. Decision-making processes are adversely affected, and when stress becomes chronic, we move from being flexible and contextualized in our responses to more rigid, habit-based systems of thinking.[52] We are less willing to compromise and hear conflicting points of view. Our cognitive abilities decrease, rendering us unable to process or remember information in the same way or effectively make decisions. Risk-based decision-making is essential to any scientific experimentation, and it is compromised by chronic stress exposure.[53]

If stress is endemic in our society and workplaces, how does this affect innovation and organizational success?

The Impact of Stress in Organizations

After seeing a study that showed the correlation between areas of the brain that are activated under threat and greater activity in individuals who are more resistant to changing their mind,[54] Lindsay realized that any proposed changes in culture and process could activate self-defense responses in many of her employees, especially if the change was poorly understood, seemed to come out of nowhere, or contradicted their beliefs. It was vital for Lindsay and other leaders to remain aware of this correlation as they developed plans for cultural change and to understand the ways in which stress might impact individuals, their collaboration dynamics, and their interactions with the system itself.

With my help, Lindsay and her team took inventory of how this played out at BPT:

After switching to a new mode of working during the 2020 pandemic and dealing with additional tasks on his plate, Phillipe complained that he was struggling to remember simple things. He was keeping up with demands, but he was conscious that it was not his best work. Stress and anxiety can influence memory loss, which is why clinical psychologists always consider these conditions when assessing someone for dementia.[55]

The pressure from senior management for late-stage development teams to succeed led Camille to feel that failure would reflect poorly on her reputation as a scientist and have adverse consequences for her career. As a result, she did not speak up about issues in the design of her vaccine trials, which incurred costs to the company to the tune of hundreds of thousands of dollars as the clinical trials got underway. Under stress, we are likely to overevaluate the threat to ourselves and act accordingly. Unfortunately, the corporate world typically does little to mitigate these threats. In fact, they often exacerbate them under the guise of motivating employees. The consequences to individuals and organizations can be severe.

As Sigrid underwent major changes in her personal life, her stress levels increased and her health suffered. Her manager noticed a decline in her work and put pressure on her to achieve. Feeling that she was letting her team down, Sigrid worked longer hours but felt that she could never catch up. She began making errors in simple protocols that she had run for years.

The business ramifications were severe, including an adverse reaction to the medication that was not identified, putting patients at risk and compromising the company's reputation.

When Matthew was faced with a decision on how to progress a product in the face of multiple unknowns and conflict in his early development virology team, his stress levels caused him to be overly cautious in making a decision. His choice to run an additional but unnecessary trial to collect more data meant that business objectives were missed. The product did not reach the market prior to a competitor's similar offering.

Rajesh faced a similar decision while chronically stressed, and his choice was to take fast action and save time but not fully evaluate the consequences. This led to a product being compromised at a later stage of development, with huge financial implications.

The impact of stress on the prefrontal cortex affects judgment and decision-making. As a result, we can be overly cautious or focus too much on potential rewards while underestimating risks. Our ability to adapt and analyze changing circumstances is reduced.[56]

Even minor stress can affect our cognitive function in the short term, as it did for Mike, a senior director at BPT and one of Lindsay's direct reports, when he replayed in his mind a putdown by Lindsay during an executive team meeting. It occupied his thoughts, reduced his attention to the task at hand, and diminished his ability to take in and process information, make decisions, and learn.[57] It also reduced the likelihood that Mike would share novel ideas in the future and therefore limited the team's creativity and affected his relationships and the team culture.

Under stress, our minds cannot fully engage with our work tasks. Our coworkers and managers often observe this, but with no explanation for the causes, the diminished performance is attributed to disengagement, laziness, or low aptitude. Stress encourages us all to fall back on our insecurities, stereotypes, and irrational ways of thinking. We react to our thoughts and emotions unconsciously, losing the ability to step back, assess the situation, and get a clear picture. We are less able to consciously choose our reactions. It is more difficult to self-regulate because our energy is redirected elsewhere, and we become less self-aware. In the moments when we most need these abilities to be functional, such as when we are under stress or in situations that demand careful thought and attention, they are most likely to be reduced.

So how are your scientists innovating now? I thought you might see that as a problem!

Investing in Teams

Beyond our individual cognitive capacities, stress and our unconscious beliefs impact how we react to and interact with others. This greatly impacts our collaborative function as a team. In fact, statistics suggest that one negative or poorly performing team member can reduce the overall functioning of an otherwise high-performing team by up to 40 percent.[58]

For organizations that require optimal employee performance and rely on teamwork and innovation for success, this is near disaster. If your biggest assets are unable to realize their potential, then the cost to the organization is significant. Organizations make a grave error when they use tight budgets as an excuse to prioritize business expenses over investing in supporting people's well-being or developing leaders who are skilled in relationships, team building, and cultivating culture. In forgoing that investment, they place additional stress on an already stressed population. In effect, they decrease the value of their largest asset—humans.

Stress and our unconscious beliefs impact how we react to and interact with others.

I understand why organizations cut costs in this fashion. It's a gray area, and it is hard to measure the financial impact of culture and well-being with standard metrics, especially in the short term. In addition, executives often possess limited understanding of the human aspects of organizational success. But human relationships and skills are increasingly recognized as important in the business world, and the data supporting these arguments continues to expand. In a digital age with a trend toward automation, the ability to be human is increasingly important. The most valued skills are human cognitive capabilities: critical thinking, relating to others, building relationships and teams, using our brains, making decisions, being creative, and solving unique problems that go beyond the reach of machines—and working collaboratively to do so.[59] However, these capabilities require healthy brain functions, so the reduction of stress is increasingly important. When we are healthy in body and mind, our contributions can be profound. When we are centered in ourselves, we can keep focus, be innovative and creative, and bring new perspectives to the table. These abilities are essential to success in an innovation environment.

Mitigating the Stress of Change

For leaders of change, the question is even bigger: *What assumptions and beliefs do my employees hold? Why might my proposed changes cause fear or stress for them?* The answers are diverse, so the solution is complex.

Once we see the way in which our personal response to stress impacts us, we need to remember that everyone has a unique experience. For example, we all have different levels of resilience to stress. What creates stress for one person might be a minor blip in the road for another. It is vital that we remember that personal reactions to stressors depend on a person's underlying biology, their experiences, the beliefs that they have formed over time, and the dynamics of their current situation. If we keep these factors in mind, then we will be less prone to judging other people's responses when they differ from ours and instead be more equipped to offer support when they need it.

Understanding these factors is crucial for any manager of people. When we transfer this knowledge to organizational change, we can see that change itself is a stressor and causes a myriad of reactions because of the unique individuals within the organization. We must understand and plan for the impact that our ideas will have on each person if we want their participation. This task will be challenging. Still, the implementation of carefully considered solutions is less time consuming, expensive, and difficult than many might expect.

Self-Awareness and the Acknowledgment of Stress

Arjun, Lindsay's COO and Head of Strategic Initiatives, always felt he had managed to keep his stress level under control. In fact, he purportedly felt energized and engaged by stress, thinking it made him more effective. But the realities reflected by his team were quite different. They recognized the stress in his face. It made them wonder, "What's wrong with the business?" It raised concerns that it was related to them. Under normal circumstances, Arjun was considered approachable, and his team enjoyed good relationships with him. However, when he was stressed, they avoided presenting issues to him. No one broached the subject of how his stress affected his team. Instead, they asked each other, "Is Arjun okay?" to see if anyone else had greater insight into what was going on and how they should approach him.

Of course, the scenario with Arjun is common because when we are under stress, most of us are less likely to be self-reflective or notice how we affect others. The stress experienced by one individual can impact psychological safety, team relations, and culture, and it can negatively impact other team members' cognitive functioning. A lack of willingness to discuss these issues, and the fact that mental health and stress are often seen as weaknesses, is a huge problem for organizations that rely on humans for their success and innovation. We need to normalize these experiences and acknowledge that everyone has unique stress responses, underlying beliefs, and assumptions and that we all experience negative emotions.

We are whole people, and we do not leave part of ourselves behind when we come to the office, even if we sometimes try to do so. The stress that we experience in our home lives encroaches on our work, and the pressures of work are taken home, impacting our families and leisure pursuits.

In an empathetic and psychologically safe environment (more on this later), people can be accepting of their entire experience as well as the experiences of others, without concern for being judged or perceived as deficient. This opens the door to address the reasons people resist change more directly because we understand the impetus that underlies the resistance.

How a Leader Takes on the Tigers

The example you set will determine a significant part of the culture and the direction of your organization. You must start with yourself. You will need to understand who you are as a leader in order to be authentic. Internal beliefs, unconscious hurdles, resistances, and stress reactions exist within you as surely as they do within the people you lead. This has to be your starting point. You must model the behaviors you hope to see in your culture and set a clear vision and strategy for change that those who follow you can believe in. When you allow others to see your authenticity, they will have confidence in your ability to lead them to a positive and desired destination.

You need to think about the culture and environment that you create, not only for the success and financial health of the organization and to attract and retain talent but because the environment we work in and the stress we experience impacts the ability of our people to succeed—as scientists, innovators, and teams.

If you want to change culture, or even processes and strategy, you need to address it at every level in the organization, starting with the individuals within it. This will make your role as a leader easier and your change faster. It will improve organizational productivity and efficiency, and it will maximize the human capabilities that are available to you. Just imagine what innovations could unfold when you enable the higher cognitive capacities of your people to work at their best and be freed from the constraints of stress.

As a leader, the example you set will determine a significant part of the culture and the direction of your organization. You must start with yourself.

This is a cultural shift. It requires a change in mindset. It requires you to lead the way and understand and act on the knowledge of what it means to be human, both for yourself and for each individual within your organization. As you work to create this environment, it is also vital to understand that humans are social by nature and that our need to belong to a group affects change, which we will explore in the next chapter.

Summary

- Our subconscious has been programmed since birth to protect us from discomfort and fear.

- Change, especially that which is imposed upon us, provokes fear and uncertainty, which leads to resistance and undermines change initiatives.

- Fear produces a stress response in our body which has not changed in the last millennium and places us in survival mode, impacting our health and cognitive abilities and provoking our unconscious defenses.

- If our brains are not functioning at their optimum, it impacts our ability for creativity, innovation, and collaboration.

- Since everyone is exposed to stress in modern life, we need to create environments that support, rather than hinder, the cognitive abilities and well-being of employees.

- For cultural change to be successful, we must thoughtfully work to overcome individual and unique fears, enabling employees to engage with, rather than resist, change.

- As a leader, you need to acknowledge your own humanity and the humanity of those you lead.

3

The Power of Social Groups

No man is an island, entire of itself; every man is a
piece of the continent, a part of the main.

—JOHN DONNE

"What did I do wrong?"

Ben was devastated by the lack of enthusiasm for his ideas and saw it as a reflection on himself. This experience changed how he behaved, as he tried to fit in and be accepted by his new team.

The behaviors people display each day are the most powerful influences on corporate culture. Sustainable change happens through gradual shifts in behaviors and through the expectations that people hold about their environment and the way their actions will be judged. To create change in culture, we must address the small things that comprise it and understand why people behave the way they do. To fully comprehend this, we must go back to the very beginning.

We Are Social Animals

We are often taught that our capacity for higher cognitive functioning makes us stand out from other mammals, but as with many things, the reality is more complex. Our brain has a dedicated system for social reasoning.[60] MRI studies show that this system is activated when we have a social focus.[61] At rest, our mind instinctively processes social situations. It dwells on other people, our past interactions with them, and what they may think of us. Matthew Lieberman, a social psychologist and neuroscientist, suggests that evolution took a bet on the fact that developing and using our social intelligence would lead to the success of the human species.[62]

The behaviors people display each day are the most powerful influences on corporate culture.

The way we evolved as humans with this social capacity means that we have an innate need to belong to a group, form connections, and relate to others. From an evolutionary perspective, this communal need makes a lot of sense. We needed to hunt together, share childcare, and protect each other from dangers.[63] Because our underlying neurology has not evolved at the rate of the world around us, communal needs continue to frame our life experiences and our behavior within organizations.

Lindsay recruited Ben for his ability to manage change. He was seen as a creative problem solver who motivated others to engage with a vision, and he created strategies and processes efficiently, moving with the demands of the market. Looking at his successes at his previous three organizations, which were all innovative new companies, Lindsay believed that Ben could propel BPT into the next stage of its vision, and he wowed her team at the interview. Here was someone dynamic, adaptable, and capable who knew their industry. Unfortunately, six months later, there were rumblings that Ben was not living up to the hype. He was doing the same old things that everyone else had done, and his potential seemed limited. What had happened?

Essentially, Ben had been absorbed and overwhelmed by the culture of a large organization. One person with a different approach and new ideas was not enough to overcome the entrenched attitudes and culture. Even others on Lindsay's leadership team who had advocated for his candidacy and argued the need for change had backed away from supporting his ideas publicly. Ben became disillusioned in the face of the battle in front of him, and with no support, he essentially gave up. Had Ben continued with his approach within a culture disapproving of change, it is likely that he would have been labeled disruptive or rebellious. His need to belong to the group was stronger than his ability to fight alone against the social norms.

This situation is not unique to Ben or a failing on his part. Culture and the norms of a group have the potential to encourage or crush you. The approval or disapproval of others significantly impacts our decisions and actions. Perhaps you remember an occasion in your own life when you altered your course because of someone else's opinion. We are profoundly affected by our social environments, and we suffer greatly if our social bonds are threatened or severed. You just have to look at the experiences of children who are bullied at school to see the impact when they are excluded from friendship groups.

Ben's experience is one example of many, and it is easy to understand how he might have felt in this particular situation. We use phrases like "It broke my heart" or "He hurt my feelings" and see them as somewhat metaphorical, but unkindness, rejection, and negative attitudes make us choose between relinquishing our ideas and being negatively labeled. This form of social pain is as real to us as physical pain:[64] Both activate our dorsal anterior cingulate cortex (dACC), which tells us we do not like pain and drives us to avoid it at all costs.[65] This neural system, which is unique to mammals, responds emotionally to the narrative of pain and is designed to keep us safe from danger.[66] It prevents us from taking actions that could result in our dismissal from the group.

Social pain is real; it impacts the ways we think and act every day. However, our inability to point to the place where it hurts, as we can with a laceration or a broken bone, leads us to dismiss the pain felt by others and even ourselves. Whether we try to ignore the pain of rejection, our brain is focused on social connections and how we fit in. Like Ben, we are motivated to avoid this experience of pain because we evolved to understand that social pain indicates a threat to our survival. Human infants, unable to obtain their basic needs alone, depend on social systems to survive. From as young as two days old, babies show signs of distress when adults adopt neutral facial expressions rather than expressive, validating ones.[67] From an evolutionary perspective, social groups and connections are a necessity, not a luxury, and are essential for our survival in the world, in the same way as food and shelter. The pain we experience is an early warning system that allows us to remain part of the group.

Groups and Divisions

Subsets form in an organization of any size, just as they did in high school. Instead of jocks and nerds, goths and the popular kids, we divide ourselves by profession or department, such as IT, sales, science, and marketing.[68] We align ourselves with coworkers who were there prior to a merger and those who are interlopers or new to the organization. We purposely categorize ourselves into teams and hierarchical structures, with broader distinctions according to gender, race, nationality, and so forth. Each group has its own subculture that exists within and forms part of the broader organizational culture.

Feeling admired, liked, or that we belong activates the striatum and other structures in the reward center of our brain.[69] Positive social feedback is pleasurable; it reinforces the behavior that elicited it. In the same way as physical and social pain share common neurocognitive processes, social rewards and physical pleasure do too.[70] We want to belong and comply with social norms not just because we fear rejection but also because as humans, we have a real preference for cooperation.[71] Our brain floods with feel-good chemicals, like oxytocin, and rewards us.[72] We want to be with people like us or who we believe like and respect us. Within an organization, these desires have implications for diversity and inclusion, but especially for cognitive diversity, the sharing of ideas and innovation, and how willing we are to appear different to our group. It is why we are drawn to groups that are like us and why we reject those that are not. Every organization is a complex animal, with a dynamic personality that shifts with changing attitudes and external pressures. To effect change and develop a cohesive culture or personality, we must understand the subtleties within which we are operating.

> **Every organization is a complex animal with a dynamic personality that shifts with changing attitudes and external pressures.**

The idea that we cooperate not just as a means to achieve selfish ends but because it brings its own rewards is contrary to how Western society tends to view the world. Based on the ideas of philosophers such as Epicurus, Hobbes, Bentham, and Hume, we assume people are motivated purely by self-interest—so much so that those with altruistic motives are devalued and stigmatized. Society has taught us to value this less. For example, nurses, teachers, and charity workers are paid less than those who focus on individual achievement and success.[73]

However, research into how our brain functions indicates that we may have this wrong. As Lieberman suggested, cooperation and being part of a group may be what enabled us to advance and succeed as a species. Being in harmony with others may take work, but evolution has predisposed us to make it a priority.

Our social nature and increased understanding of these concepts should impact how we think about structuring organizations, diversity, inclusion, and how we create environments free of social threats so we can bring our whole selves to the table. Despite humans evolving to be social animals, the institutions and organizations in which people spend their lives are not tailored to meet these needs.[74] Instead of focusing on individual motivations and rewards, we must also consider the social motivations of individuals who desire to align as groups and the impact these decisions have on their thoughts and behaviors.

Belonging and Conformity

The self is much more socially created than we might think. In the West, we tend to focus on the individual, thinking of our actions, thoughts, and behaviors as distinct from other people's.[75] The truth is, we constantly evaluate what we believe others think of us, assessing whether we will remain part of the group or be excluded and basing our decisions and actions on those assessments. Neurologically, the medial prefrontal cortex (between our eyes) constantly reflects on ourselves[76] and others.[77] It ensures that we hold similar beliefs and values as those around us because one of our primary survival mechanisms is social harmony. This instinctive guidance makes us gravitate toward people with whom we share commonalities. Since these associations feel safe, we find it easier to be accepted, and this helps ensure our survival.

Whenever we are uncertain, we look to the group to inform us. Often, this is a smart strategy because it allows us to learn quickly, but there is also a downside. To fit in, we may conform to ideas that are incorrect or inferior to avoid being excluded or seen as different. The Asch paradigms in the 1950s demonstrated the impact of conformity within social settings, where even when they knew an answer was patently incorrect, subjects felt unable to resist conforming to the group consensus. Another famous example captured on a *Candid Camera* episode in 1962 showed how when people entered an elevator with everyone facing the rear, they followed suit.[78] The tendency of groups to make decisions that preserve the status quo is commonly known as groupthink and presents obvious disadvantages in the world of research and innovation where we want to encourage cognitive diversity and promote inclusion of differing ideas.[79]

Leading and Following

Leaders play a vital role in groups. Although leadership research traditionally focuses on the best qualities of a leader, this is perhaps the wrong focus. When we think about social groups and our need to belong, it becomes much more apparent that the question should be, *Why do we follow people? What is the purpose of a leader, and what do they provide to people at the level of fundamental needs?*

As humans evolved within social groups, leadership and followership became adaptive strategies to manage risk and coordinate activities to the mutual benefit of the group, such as hunting, defense, and collective movement.[80] In these small societies, leaders had a differential influence on the choices and direction of the group.[81] But since leadership was situational and temporary, leaders were chosen based on skills and experience for the task at hand. It was not about dominance or coercion, and following was always voluntary.[82] As group members, we evolved to be flexible to follow or lead as the situation demanded and according to the current needs of the group and its members.[83] The success of humans has in part been tied to the natural selection of our social ability to coordinate and follow the right leaders in the right circumstances.[84]

Since the advent of agriculture some 12,000 years ago and the ability to store crops and wealth, leaders became more dominant, and the power differentials changed.[85] Modern society has exacerbated this shift, with groups becoming much larger and including corporations and even nations. We have set up hierarchical systems where leaders are permanent and not context dependent. Still, while societal structures have altered, this is too short a time in evolutionary terms to affect the neurology and adaptive psychological processes that evolved during the previous million years or so.[86]

Followers in organizations now have little say in the selection of leaders and following has become less voluntary. In shifting this way, we are negating the very processes that led to our survival as a species: the ability to be flexible in our choices to lead or follow, select the best leaders for a task, or cooperate for competitive advantage. We follow leaders when we believe they can help us achieve our goals and because they provide a sense of belonging and stability.[87] They have greater power to decide whether we can remain members of the group. If we did not choose our leader and do not trust or feel accepted by them, then we become anxious about remaining in the group. This anxiety increases our stress, affects our engagement, and reduces our commitment to the common goal.

Lindsay had observed that her CEO, Joshua, tended to micromanage under pressure. She recognized that this tendency increased the likelihood of her withdrawing or disengaging and that it had a similar impact on her team unless she actively shielded them from his actions. A CEO like Joshua, who reverts to control and command dominance behaviors when under stress, in effect removes the ability of the group to succeed through the use of all their skills. Lindsay compared Joshua to her colleague, Helen, the Chief Marketing Officer (CMO). Even under pressure, Helen stepped back to acknowledge the skillsets of her group members and allowed them to step forward to lead in their areas of expertise. Lindsay could see a clear difference in the level of creativity, engagement, and progress toward goals between these groups, with Helen's team outperforming Joshua's in every aspect. Employees' needs are rarely considered from a social perspective.

Instead, the focus is on the needs of the organization or individual career prospects. But employees, like humans throughout history, look to leaders to learn the skills of leadership and to understand appropriate group norms.[88]

Thinking about leadership from an evolutionary perspective, it is important to acknowledge that being a leader is not about hierarchy or dominance. It is about knowing yourself, knowing what you have to offer in any situation, and judging whether now is the time to step forward and lead or to allow someone else to take the reins. Leading is about ensuring that everyone feels a sense of belonging and creating safety and security to enable people to perform optimally. It is understanding that belonging is not the same as fitting in. Rather, belonging is about being accepted for who you are and what you bring to a group.

Social Animals in an Innovation Environment

Innovation typically relies on human interaction.[89] It is a social process and is affected by our desires to belong, to be respected, and to maintain the status quo. But the very nature of innovation goes against the status quo because it brings disruption and change. If we avoid intellectual conflict, we avoid bringing new knowledge and ideas to the table and stifle creativity. Often, intellectual conflict threatens us and brings about social conflict, so we avoid it. This can have serious business consequences, resulting in delays, increased risk, terminations, and loss of time and money.[90] If our brains evolved to fear exclusion from a group or judgment by others, then we have some work to do to overcome these factors.

Lindsay recognized that there had been occasions when she inadvertently created social conflict. For example, when Mike, one of her key chemistry experts, had spoken up with an idea that did not seem to fit her strategy, Lindsay was quick to dismiss it during the meeting. Reflecting afterward on her actions, she realized that Mike's suggestion was actually a creative solution to their problem. It had been her own insecurity about her expertise and worry about others' judgments of her knowledge that led her to respond impulsively. Lindsay realized that her dismissiveness left Mike feeling humiliated. As an introvert, he would probably be less open to speaking up in public settings in future. Without his expert contributions, the possibilities for innovation were reduced. Lindsay also realized that her whole team witnessed this interaction. Would it discourage the others from speaking up in future meetings? What did it say to them about her openness to new ideas?

The very nature of innovation goes against the status quo because it brings disruption and change.

People rarely discuss this kind of social conflict or disagreement. When an argument between two of her direct reports surfaced during a meeting that hurt feelings and generated emotional responses throughout the group, Lindsay was quick to shut it down and suggest that they revisit the issue rather than attempting to understand the motivations behind the disagreement. Like Lindsay, most leaders are not comfortable with the "emotional stuff." If we do not know how to fix it, we are tempted to brush it under the carpet and pretend that it does not matter. But these conflicts have serious social repercussions. They leave people feeling alienated from each other, ostracized, or resented by the team for creating a problem or for being too emotional. People are then less likely to contribute, take risks or speak up about problems. Social conflict feels very personal because it triggers our internal self-judgments and our worries about how others perceive us.[91]

Being social in nature, we do not forget negative interactions. Our brains analyze and dwell on them, and they come back as anxiety the next time that we want to disagree. Our stress response is activated, and we may avoid disagreeing because of the negative consequences that we previously experienced. This stress affects our relationships with others who were involved because we have our own interpretation of how they judged the event. It might be a small event in the context of a global organization's operations, but it can have a profound effect. Because culture is created by the small things people say and do each day, the ripple effect is far greater than the event itself. These events get into our unconscious minds and create the real organizational culture, the rules that say, "This is what happens when you do X."

At BPT, despite openly promoting the introduction of an innovative culture that is receptive to new ideas and open discourse, the "real rules" of the organization led people to believe that there was instead a culture of blame. Because timelines and goals were the priorities and success was linked with performance-related pay, fear became a motivator. When this happens, innovation fails. People stop speaking out because failure is met with negative consequences, and risk is avoided rather than treated as a learning opportunity. At BPT, this dynamic was devastating to the iterative process of innovation and the culture of continuous improvement that leadership aspired to develop.

We must be aware of the subtleties of how our minds interpret the world around us and ask ourselves if our actions match our words and how we undermine our own best intentions. Understanding the value that our brains unconsciously place on our social interactions and belonging demonstrates the need to incorporate this, not just into the process and procedures, but also the ways we measure performance and value the journey as much as the destination or goal. Often, what we do along the way is more relevant to our overall success than achieving a planned outcome.

Nothing exists for itself alone, but only in relation to other forms of life.

—CHARLES DARWIN

When you examine the causes of failure for any major organization, you see a reduction in intellectual conflict or friction. This typically correlates with a lack of psychological safety within the organization's culture and an avoidance of social conflict. Over the decade prior to the arrival of Satya Nadella, Microsoft ceased to challenge itself. It was an internally competitive culture that feared failure and sought to be right, which created fears of social consequences and prevented healthy debate, so innovation declined.[92] As Kodak focused on their core business and avoided disruption to achieve their goals, they missed the changing market desires.[93]

Ultimately, their failure was avoiding risk, ignoring diverse views, and discouraging input from varying perspectives. Traditional management approaches, the usual success metrics, and methods of rewarding performance are the enemies of innovation because they instill unconscious fears and adherence to unproductive group norms.

> **Traditional management approaches, the usual success metrics, and methods of rewarding performance are the enemies of innovation.**

For successful change, we must consider individual, social, and cultural influences and understand how people really see and respond to the world around them. We need to create an environment in which innovation and disruption become the norm without being blocked by our individual and social fears of exclusion, judgment, or punishment. Groups are powerful. They are committed to maintaining their status quo and to repelling any outside threats. Change threatens both groups and the individuals within them, activating the stress response.

We often think that personalities are difficult to change, so if a culture within a small or large group is similar to its personality, then we certainly have a challenge ahead. However, like personality, culture is not fixed. It develops and evolves over time, and it remains open to adaptation. The challenge then becomes, *How do we motivate a group to change without activating defensive responses that make them resist the change?* We'll discuss this in more depth in Part Three.

Summary

- We have evolved to be social animals and belong to groups because they ensure our survival.

- We constantly evaluate what others think of us, and we want to fit in, which can lead to us conforming to group norms.

- Rejection causes the same intensity of pain as a physical injury, and we are motivated to avoid it because it warns us we may be excluded from the group.

- Social groups are motivated to maintain harmony and their status quo, which can result in decreased cognitive diversity.

- Every group has a culture and there can be many groups within an organization that interact to create common understandings that influence your organizational culture as a whole.

- To engage people and create change, leaders must reduce the social threats, utilize the influence they have within a group, and enable others to take the lead as required by circumstances.

- Behavior has a powerful influence on culture. To be successful, organizations need to design environments that take into consideration the social motivations of the people within them.

4 | How Our Brains and Beliefs Limit Change

The news that reaches your consciousness is incomplete and often not to be relied on.

—SIGMUND FREUD

Our brain develops at an incredible rate during our early years. For the first few years, while we interact with our caregivers and the world around us, more than a million new neural connections are created every second.[94]

From our earliest experiences, we begin to form expectations about how the world will respond to us. Is it safe or unsafe? Can people be trusted to meet our needs? Each time Lindsay cried as a baby, her mother picked her up to soothe or feed her. These interactions created a positive emotional relationship and helped her to develop resilience. Sam had repeated negative experiences with his caregivers, who were unable to meet his needs, at this early age he began to expect negative behaviors from others.

Each experience these babies had formed neural connections in their brains. Repeated similar experiences over time strengthened the synaptic connections and formed pathways in their brains, allowing them to predict responses from the world and form beliefs. Going forward, it altered their perceptions and how they interpreted incoming information. Exposed to the same event today, Lindsay and Sam will interpret and respond differently because of their expectations and beliefs about the world.

We are bombarded with information every minute of every day through what we see, hear, think, and feel. An average adult has over 6,000 thoughts a day and potentially many thousands more depending on how we define a thought. This activity is registered by the brain and neural pathways are created, forming many of our major beliefs.[95] We must have a way to sort and process this information. Our brain helps us do so by creating categories and beliefs and forming meaning. By making these connections in the brain, we build an explanatory framework for interpreting the world.[96] But this can cause problems.

Most of our core beliefs are formed in early childhood while our brains are developing and absorbing information at the greatest rate. Unfortunately, children do not have capacity for logic and reason, leaving a lot of room for error in how they understand the world and develop their beliefs.[97] As a baby, Sam was unable to understand that his mother did not respond positively to him on a consistent basis because she suffered from postnatal depression and had no help in caring for him. He could only learn that the world was inconsistent and unable to meet his basic needs and that others were unreliable, which made him feel unsafe and sad.

When Lindsay was six years old and her parents argued shortly after telling her she needed to work hard at school, she connected the wrong dots and thought, "If I do better at school, then my parents won't fight." This set her up for a lifetime of always needing to work harder, assuming that she was not good enough. Now consider David, whose family loved his intelligence but questioned him for getting an answer wrong. At age eight, he knew that if he had studied harder and gotten it right, then his parents would love him more.

It is easy for adults to see these errors in logic, but for children, that is not possible. As all new information is processed in relation to what we already know and believe, most of us go through our lives basing our decisions and reactions on this faulty data, which became hardwired into our brains during childhood.

The Automation of Thinking

Remember when you first learned how to drive? There were so many things to concentrate on—check your mirrors, change gear, depress the clutch with your left foot but use your right on the brake, pay attention to the road, don't turn the wheel when you turn your head, and stay on the correct side of the road! Today, with years of practice, you do not need to concentrate as hard on these steps because the processes are now automated.[98] You can give more attention to whatever is happening around you—listen to music or plan what you will do when you arrive at your destination. By automating and creating strong neural pathways for the processes involved in driving, your brain has freed up space and energy to work on other things.

We do this in all aspects of our lives, from forming our beliefs to categorizing events, people, and groups. Most of the time, reducing the brain's energy requirements is a great strategy because it allows us more capacity to learn and grow. However, there are times when this is less helpful. By categorizing, we stereotype, and we automate those thoughts so that unless we pay attention, these biases and actions happen unconsciously and automatically. Moving from the United Kingdom to the United States, I occasionally found myself wondering why some idiot was driving toward me on the wrong side of the road. In these moments, it was less than helpful that my brain had automated left-side driving. Rather quickly, I was forced to bring that assumption into awareness and recategorize myself as the idiot on the wrong side.

Automation is generally a useful process that helps us make sense of the world to be more efficient with our time, thoughts, and energy.[99] Still, we need to be conscious of when it happens. We must acknowledge that we all make assumptions about the world and other people based on our prior knowledge and experience but that those assumptions may employ faulty logic.

The Influence of Society and Groups

As it grows, our brain learns and develops based on our experience and finds ways to make sense of the world. But at our core, we remain social animals. We do not develop in isolation, and our brains have evolved to constantly process our beliefs about others and how they perceive us. Our earliest experiences come from our caregivers, but as we grow, we are exposed to the world, and our beliefs develop based on the culture in which we live. We adopt popular stereotypes in society, assume the beliefs of our family, absorb the messages we see on TV, and learn through our emotional responses to whatever feels good or bad.[100]

Our brains have evolved to constantly process our beliefs about others and how they perceive us.

The majority of what we believe is unconscious and beyond our immediate awareness. But conscious or not, our brains accept our beliefs as true, and our beliefs provide the basis by which we understand and react to the world.[101] These beliefs and assumptions enable us to put our experiences into wider contexts and give them meaning. They enable us to place ourselves in the world and assess how we should behave and react in order to belong, which as we know, we value as a species. We want to share beliefs, as shared beliefs help define group norms, and they help us understand our identity and support our belonging to the group.

Our genetics may serve as a blueprint for our brain, but our environment and experiences determine what grows.[102] We are biased to build on our existing beliefs, faulty or not. Our beliefs are consolidated within the neural networks and the physical structures of our brain. Therefore, as you might expect, they are difficult to change. We are predisposed to see what we expect to see, to take in information that fits with our existing beliefs, and to build on our existing networks. Even with objectively convincing evidence, deeply entrenched beliefs are resistant to change. A group of psychologists discovered this in the 1950s when they infiltrated a cult that believed that the world would end on December 21, 1954. Very few cult members questioned their beliefs, even in response to the compelling evidence that they were still in existence on December 22, 1954, and beyond.[103]

If people can maintain faulty beliefs even about factual information that can be verified, like the cult members did, then how easy is it for people to hold on to incorrect or ambiguous beliefs—especially those about ourselves—that we cannot easily verify? The situation resembles David's feeling that he needed to prove himself right in order to be worthwhile and accepted by his family or Lindsay's fears that she was not good enough. These long-standing beliefs, formed erroneously during childhood but cemented into our brains by repeated experiences that we accept as confirmatory evidence, are hard to change, but it is possible. Often, the biggest obstacle to change is our own fear. Our unconscious mind recognizes our fear and works hard to remain within our comfort zone, secure in our long-standing beliefs and assumptions about the world.

These beliefs persist throughout our lives, usually on an unconscious, automated level, informing or interfering with everything we do, unless we specifically act to change them. Each of us has to ask, *What assumptions and preconceptions do I hold about myself, others, and situations that thwart my progress? How do they limit the ways in which I interact with the world and limit my self-confidence and my potential?*

Inside Your Mind

It is Monday morning, and Jane is in a meeting with her peers. They are a diverse group, and she knows some participants better than others. The topic of cultural change arises, which captures Jane's attention. She listens carefully and feels that she has some valuable input on the subject, even though it falls outside of her area of expertise. She hesitates and feels conflicted about whether to speak up or stay quiet.

To understand how our brain makes sense of these situations, let's take a journey through Jane's internal processing.[104] First, Jane turns inward, considering, "Who am I? What do I want to do in this situation?" She reflects on herself and knows she is someone who likes to be helpful. She believes her information could be useful to others, and as such, she wants to speak up and knows she has typically felt good when she has done this in the past.

"But wait," her brain interjects. "You want to be liked, remember? You don't want to be thrown out of the group, nor do you want people to think negatively of you." Jane wonders how the others might react to her speaking up. Are they going to judge her? Will it go well?

She scans the room and tries to predict everyone's responses. She wonders, "What would I do if I were them?" She predicts Chan and François will react positively and engage in a conversation. She assumes Rebecca will be critical, thinking it's not Jane's area of expertise. And she worries about the response from Pedro—the leader of this team and her boss. "Will Pedro perceive my comments as contradictory to his own and react defensively, or will he welcome the suggestion?"

Jane's amygdala, located deep in the center of her brain, shouts out, "It's a risk! Do you really want to do this?" Jane notices a surge of anxiety as this possible threat initiates her physiological stress responses. Her heart races, and she starts to feel hot. She worries the group may not find it acceptable for her to speak up; it's not the norm in this group for people to comment outside their own area of expertise. She remembers how embarrassed she felt that time she spoke up and Pedro dismissed her comments in front of the entire group. Her brain thus warns her, "It is definitely a bad idea to say anything! What if you stutter because you are anxious? That will just confirm what you already know Pedro thinks, which is that women are less confident and not as good at their jobs.[105] That could affect your promotion."

In the moment, Jane vacillates between the positives and negatives of sharing her ideas with the group. As she makes assumptions about their reactions, she fears being rejected and possibly excluded, and the stress she experiences undermines her confidence. It's easy to see how a choice to hold back could limit her potential.

During coaching, Jane and I explored her tendency to hold back or worry about the reactions of her team. Armed with this self-awareness, Jane was able to recognize the conflict in her mind. She was therefore able to reflect on her beliefs and the accuracy of her assumptions in order to override her automatic unconscious reaction to stay silent. Instead, she took steps to calm her stress response and make a calculated, conscious decision about how to act.

Without this self-awareness and ability to pause and reflect, Jane would have been at the whim of her unconscious mind, reacting to the beliefs and assumptions embedded within her neural networks. It is true for us all that when we feel stress or perceive a threat, we lose much of our ability to be rational or self-reflective, and we can struggle to resist our evolutionary and physiological predispositions. Ultimately, the unconscious mind exposes us to self-sabotage and can cause us to behave in ways that we later regret.

At some level, every human is concerned with self-image because we are social animals.[106] We feel the need to constantly manage our identity. We manage it internally to feel good about ourselves and externally to ensure the image we present to the world is one that our family, colleagues, and bosses find acceptable and will keep us connected to them. Jane's example demonstrates the complexity of our decision-making and the influence that our unconscious beliefs and assumptions can have on our thoughts and actions.

Since our brains continually process information in this manner, you can begin to appreciate the complexities involved in the way that people think, feel, and choose to behave in any given situation. To change any part of this process, we must be able to see it clearly. Since it happens largely within our unconscious mind, the change is hard to make. For most of us, we react instinctively to the part that shouts the loudest, that calls to our underlying fears. This is not something someone else can change for you. It is an internal process that needs to be brought into conscious awareness for change to occur. Often, we need support to gain that insight, and we certainly need to take the time to reflect. In Chapter Eight, we will think about some of the ways you can begin to do this.

If you want to transform an organization, it is essential that you create the conditions under which people are able to change.

It is essential to acknowledge that people can only make these changes themselves. You cannot force them to change, at least not in any meaningful or sustainable way. If you want to transform an organization, it is essential that you create the conditions under which people are able to change.

We already know a few tendencies: people want to belong to groups and are likely to follow and emulate leaders whom they admire. Our brain automates much of our thinking to help us quickly make sense of the world, and this can lead to faulty logic. Everyone has different life experiences and sees the world through their own lenses.

We cannot know the workings of another person's mind, but we can understand that stress impacts individuals in ways that are unhelpful to building successful and innovative organizations. If you want to effect change, then you must understand that everyone has beliefs and assumptions that may cause them to feel threatened or removed from their comfort zone, and this may alter their behavior.

Resistance is a natural human response that is deeply lodged within the physical structures of our brains. Since culture is based on the small things that people do and say every day and these small things are affected by our beliefs, assumptions, and evolutionary predispositions, we must consider these tendencies in order to create healthy conditions for transformation. By working to increase employee well-being, reduce stress in organizations, and become leaders people want to emulate, as well as considering how to alter inhibiting beliefs, help employees recognize the faulty logic in their thinking, and introduce ideas without creating fear, we can help people engage effectively with cultural transformation. This will support not only individual and cultural change but also innovation and organizational success.

Moving forward with this idea, we need to question what motivates people to grow and develop and what factors might contribute to a culture in which this is increasingly possible.

Human Growth and Development

Meeting Our Needs

Under his hierarchical theory of motivation, Abraham Maslow's basic premise is that people must satisfy the needs of each level before they can advance to fulfilling the needs of subsequent levels.[107] Without having our basic needs met, such as food, water, and shelter, it is difficult for us to dedicate energy toward more abstract concepts, such as self-fulfillment. In earlier ages, humans primarily focused on meeting their basic needs at the lower levels of this hierarchy, and little time was available for their broader contributions to the world. In modern times, technological and societal advances have afforded people more time to think about themselves, their place in the world, and achieving their potential.

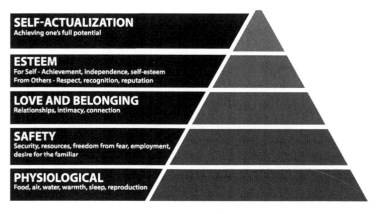

Maslow's hierarchy of needs

As a senior leader of a large global company, Lindsay had a secure and well-paid job. She was married, with a supportive family, and she was easily able to provide for their basic needs. At work, she felt respected by her colleagues, and her career was on an upward trajectory. She had time to focus on her personal development and fulfilling her self-actualization.

Sometimes, however, we get in our own way.

How We Sabotage Ourselves

During my coaching sessions with Lindsay, she highlighted that there were certain situations in which she did not speak up as effectively as she had intended. As we began to untangle this discrepancy, we found that it happened most frequently in meetings where her superiors were present. We needed to explore the reasons she communicated effectively in situations with peers, subordinates, or external partners but less so with her superiors. As with Jane, there was the potential here for Lindsay to self-sabotage if she did not pause and reflect on the situation. But let's take a different view and examine this scenario from Maslow's perspective as this can give us more clues to developing environments that support individuals and change processes.

Lindsay loved her job, which gave her personal fulfillment. She even found stressful situations energizing, as she perceived them as fun problems to solve. In this respect, Lindsay was moving toward fulfilling her potential at level five of Maslow's hierarchy of needs and was enjoying the process.

So where did the problem lie? Lindsay acknowledged that she wanted respect from her CEO, Joshua, and for him to acknowledge her performance. At times, it seemed that he failed to do so. Her frustration triggered internal, unconscious beliefs that had developed during her childhood that said that she wasn't good enough. Lindsay worried, "What if Joshua thinks this too?" If he could see that she wasn't good enough, then she would be cast out of the executive team and maybe even fired. Suddenly, level four of the hierarchy was abruptly removed as she doubted Joshua's respect for her. Lindsay's ability to perform her job and fulfill her potential diminished because this unconscious belief held her back from speaking up in her usual confident manner.

In this situation, all of Lindsay's natural human fears about belonging and staying within the group were activated. She assumed that it was better to say nothing in case what she said was wrong. Delving deeper, we found that her fear of being fired destabilized her sense of belonging and threatened her safety, security, and role as her family's provider. Lindsay's stress response was now activated; her cognitive abilities of logic and reason were dampened. Her ancient brain foretold a negative dramatic conclusion in which she was cast out of her job, her family no longer valued her, and she ended up living alone on the streets while her children starved. In less than the blink of an eye, Lindsay's unconscious mind had sabotaged her with her core belief that she was not good enough. It had transported her to the lowest level of Maslow's hierarchy, where even her basic needs were in doubt.

Of course, if deconstructed, Lindsay could see her thinking was ludicrous. One wrong utterance in a meeting would not outweigh everything else that she had done or change what Joshua thought of her. The likelihood that her imagined chain of events would *actually* happen was remote.

But—and this is a huge but—**your brain doesn't know this.**

Typically, you are not consciously aware of your ludicrous thoughts. Neither Lindsay nor Jane in our earlier example could change their brain's automatic reaction or these thoughts without working to understand what was happening beneath the surface and bringing it to conscious awareness. We are almost always our own worst critic. To make change, we must acknowledge and become aware that our thinking at the unconscious level is shaped by faulty data that stems from our childhood experiences or evolutionary predispositions. Admittedly, these reactions would be hard for you to change in each individual in your organization. However, when we understand human needs and motivations, we can develop positive work environments that allow people to achieve their potential and develop mutually beneficial relationships.

For example, if you know that you didn't sleep well last night, then you can cut yourself some slack when you overreact to a coworker's comment and make amends. When Frankie is unusually argumentative, his coworkers might question whether something else is going on in his personal life rather than reacting defensively. When all the employees in our organization complain about the changes that we are promoting, we can ask ourselves, "Why are they resisting? Do they understand what it means for them?" When Sanjeev doesn't speak up during times of organizational unrest, we can wonder, "Is he concerned about his job security?"

The reality for all of us is that we can move up and down Maslow's hierarchical levels within milliseconds. When we understand how our brains want to meet our needs and the order of priority, as well as understanding how our unconscious beliefs and social desires lead us to self-sabotage or resist change, we gain insight into how we can develop organizational processes and culture to support the development of ourselves and others. In Chapter Seven, we will examine what this might look like within your organization because in order to achieve our potential—or to support and develop the potential of others—we must be at our optimal selves, and this requires being in an environment that facilitates that.

Taking care of ourselves and feeling whole does not detract from the needs of the organization.

Being torn apart by the demands of an uncaring system or corporation that forces us to participate in their desired programs can lead to losing ourselves. We can lose our voice, our perspective, and often our empathy as we are caught up in the demands and pressures of leading a business in a capitalist system. We forget what makes the business function—people. And sometimes we forget that we are people too. It is vital that we find our voice and stand up for our needs. Taking care of ourselves and feeling whole does not detract from the needs of the organization.

Beyond individuals, we must consider that the actions each of us take affect how others feel and respond. Because culture is created through behaviors, these actions have a huge impact on the environment we create and work in together every day. Healthy people and relationships contribute to the success of any organization in a myriad of ways, and it is worth placing our attention on these factors.

Putting It Together

It's important to realize that our life experiences of environments or people that left us feeling judged, humiliated, and fearful have a long-lasting impact on our brain development, sense of self, and worldview. Everyone has these types of experiences, to greater or lesser degrees, repeatedly throughout their lives. They leave emotions ingrained on the psyche and are lodged deeply within the neural networks of the unconscious mind. Each experience builds on the previous one, creating connections between the neural structures and strengthening the link between experience and emotion. Repeated experiences also strengthen habitual reactions and strategies for protecting our self-image, however faulty the logic may be.

As you try to change culture or behavior, you challenge strong connections that were built into people's brains over many years. It is unrealistic to expect that people will change instantaneously, even with compelling evidence. Resistance still occurs in the mind—even when evidence is accepted on an intellectual level and change is desired. It takes time to change the internal workings of the mind and the physical structures of the brain. In real life, individual thinking, concerns, and resistance to change are entangled with social needs; together, they are part of larger webs of organizational life, culture, and society. Knowing that the foundation of strong cognitive capabilities is emotional well-being, social competence, and belonging helps us understand why we need to consider the human needs of employees. These needs are especially critical for life science innovation, which demands that our scientists use the fullest capacity of their brains to achieve success. We must create a culture that supports individual change as well as organizational change, which we will explore in the chapters that follow.

Summary

- We create neural networks during childhood that form the basis of our beliefs, understanding, and assumptions about the world throughout our lifetime.

- Our beliefs and assumptions are often inaccurate because we formed them as children when we lacked the ability to reason about our experiences.

- Our brain automates many processes and beliefs to conserve energy and help us make sense of the world efficiently. This automation can prevent self-awareness around our thoughts and actions and lead us to form stereotypes.

- We are predisposed to seek out confirmatory evidence for our existing beliefs, and we often act on faulty data that we rarely question.

- Unless we are self-aware, we are guided by our unconscious beliefs, and they influence how we interpret and react to the world around us.

- Our desire to meet our needs, preserve our self-image, and belong combines with our unconscious beliefs and assumptions, which can lead us to self-sabotage.

- For cultural change in an organization, we must understand the complexity that exists in each human within our organization. If we hope to create change, then we must work with, rather than against, our human tendencies.

PART TWO

EXPECTATIONS AND THE ELEMENTS OF SUCCESSFUL INNOVATION CULTURES

5 | What to Expect on the Journey Ahead

Sometimes, I've believed as many as six impossible things before breakfast.

—LEWIS CARROLL (THE QUEEN OF HEARTS)

"It's impossible!" declared Lindsay, throwing up her hands in frustration. "There are so many factors! How can we possibly know or address everything in each individual's mind, let alone everything affecting groups or the organization at large?"

Lindsay's response is understandable. It is the one that I see most often from leaders, which they occasionally verbalize but more often express through the silence that follows our conversation on this subject. People intrinsically understand the concepts that affect change and appreciate their relevance, but these concepts can feel impossible to tackle. Leaders often feel overwhelmed and find it easier to stick to the tried-and-tested approaches, even if they acknowledge that these approaches failed to work in the past.

Sure, it is a little challenging! However, I believe it is a challenge that scientists are particularly well equipped to take on—and Lindsay was no exception. Her momentary frustration quickly dissipated into her usual solution-focused mindset. She saw that changing culture was similar to the evolution of any other scientific endeavor:

1. Observe an issue. In Lindsay's case, our culture is not supporting our desired outcomes as an R&D organization.

2. Question how to address the issue and what new knowledge is needed to do so.

3. Form a hypothesis.

4. Make a prediction.

5. Test and iterate!

This is what scientists do every day, yet they rarely apply these skills to solving human issues within their organizations.

Growth and Resistance

Lindsay knew that innovation was a key focus of most businesses in the twenty-first century, and certainly a key focus for the scientific R&D world. She also knew that change is a vital aspect of any innovation. How much an organization, its leadership, and its employees are willing to embrace change often decides whether disruptive growth and innovation are possible. This is a question Lindsay was prepared to ask of herself and her people.

As we learned earlier, at a neurobiological level, we are all designed to resist change that provokes uncertainty. Perhaps you can relate to this notion. If you have ever tried to implement change, then you probably know what it is like to hit a wall of resistance. Maybe the resistance occurred at the outset, with expressed disagreement toward the process; or maybe it was subtle, with progress being undermined in small ways. *Have you ever encountered resistance when everyone seemed enthusiastic and headed in the same direction only to see the desired outcome elude you?*

At BPT, each successive change left the employees increasingly fatigued and jaded. During my tenure in the United Kingdom's National Health Service, one of the world's largest employers, the resistance to change was apparent to everyone who worked there. With a change in government policy occurring roughly every four years, transformations were drawn up and set in place just in time for a new administration to change it. Employees had come to believe they just needed to keep working as usual and maintain the status quo because attempted change was too grandiose to find short-term success. The resulting negativity within the system bred more resistance to future ideas or changes. No matter how good the innovation appeared, employees inevitably reacted with eye rolls and skeptical attitudes of "Here we go again." This poor reception is the case in most organizations, even if it is not apparent on the surface. Even organizations that appear to embrace change must manage the internal resistance felt by individuals and groups.

Appreciating Complexity

It is impossible to apply a simple model to the goal of changing societal or organizational behavior. By its very nature, change within human systems is always complex. Solutions and strategies for change must embrace this complexity by recognizing the unique characteristics of each system or organization and tailor strategies to those environments. Solutions must fit the needs of the system within which they are intended to operate.

I saw this clearly in my training as a clinical psychologist, where we trained in integrative approaches to psychological theory and practice. We used multilevel clinical perspectives and placed an emphasis on the social determinants of health and culture. As a result, I have a breadth of knowledge across a variety of domains. Although I have deep knowledge and expertise in some areas, I also have a broad perspective that permits the cross-pollination of ideas and concepts from other fields of knowledge.

I can adapt this breadth of knowledge quickly in the face of change. This versatility has been invaluable to me throughout my career as a psychologist because it helps me view the world from differing perspectives and understand the ways that others perceive their own reality. This ability to adapt and be open to new ways of thinking and perceiving the world is as essential in innovation and today's business world as it is in psychology.

To achieve change, we must take a broad view to consider how systems interact at every level—from individual neurology, unconscious beliefs, and relationships, to the influence of society and world cultures. This broad view is analogous to how Narinder, as a medicinal chemist, first needs to understand the underlying molecular, biochemical, and genetic mechanisms that lead to disease before he can apply his knowledge and experience to designing solutions that address real-world problems. If we do not look at the cultural and societal context along with the behaviors and neuropsychology of individuals and teams that sit within the system, then we cannot hope to successfully create change.

Be Proactive, Not Reactive

In order to survive, an organism must adapt as its environment changes. If it waits too long or the environment changes too suddenly, then extinction lies on the horizon.[108] Similarly, an organization survives by its collective response to stimuli within its environment.[109] If you respond too slowly, you risk falling behind your competitors. Hasty action or failure to anticipate future market demands are equally recipes for disaster.

Many know that change is a constant, but they do not know what changes to expect. To address this uncertainty, organizations must develop the key attributes of flexibility and adaptability to facilitate change as needed. However, you also have the power to influence the way in which an environment changes. To do so, you must engage the brain of every person involved to ensure that neurologically they are trained for flexibility and adaptation. Each individual response to change will determine the speed and efficacy of your cultural adaptation or evolution.

Unfortunately, most companies only change when forced to do so. They ignore environmental shifts and then urgently rush to adopt large changes in desperate attempts at self-preservation. Previously, we explored how sudden change or change that employees find meaningless establishes a pattern of resistance. Change can be so much easier if organizations forgo this eleventh-hour scramble and instead develop a flexible culture that is open to new ideas and cultivates employees who are resilient and adaptable. The cultural change process itself presents an opportunity for your organization to model new, aspirational ways of working with your employees. Through that process, you afford people a lived experience of the organizational dynamics that enable both scientific innovation and business success.

Organizations must develop the key attributes of flexibility and adaptability to facilitate change as needed.

Lindsay understood and emphasized the importance of culture within her organization, but through this process, she had learned to expect resistance, especially in times of stress and pressure. For example, people who agreed with her ideas during the "good times" retreated under financial or time constraints of the business and left her feeling isolated. With stress and competing demands at the forefront, dedication to cultural change often plummets. Losing sight of priorities is easy if you are not mindful of your end goal. With pressure from management and the markets, we are prone to fall back on old habits, and we prioritize business issues that are traditionally perceived as more important.

However, the world has changed and continues to do so at an unprecedented rate, and to succeed, we must prioritize people. Diverse thinking, higher cognitive skills, and emotional intelligence are essential components of an innovation environment and of agile organizations. In Lindsay's situation, the creation of an adaptable, innovative culture required her to be mindful of where she placed her focus. This is not to say that we ignore other aspects of organizational life and success. We simply should not allow the human dimensions to fall off our radar.

Change Takes Time

As Lindsay came to understand the mindsets of the people within her organization and their internal resistances, as well as her own, she began to truly appreciate that sustainable cultural change takes time. It begins with the small changes that build confidence in leadership. She realized that organizations must embrace change at the highest levels, and all members of leadership must demonstrate it consistently. As we saw in Chapter Three, evolution predisposes us to feelings of belonging that are satisfied by group membership. If we fail to acknowledge this facet of human nature, then change at a cultural level is tough. We are motivated to follow leaders who can benefit the group, garner our respect, and role model aspirational behavior. Great leaders are set apart by knowledge, the ability to learn, and the willingness to do things differently. You must start within yourself before focusing outward into the organization.

More than any other area of change, culture is one where the group's acceptance of ideas, new patterns of behavior, and norms is vital, and leaders have a valuable role to play. Take the time to develop a growth culture, where people can work in a psychologically safe environment that fosters flexibility and adaptability. Facilitating this environment should be your organization's first step to provide a platform for people to embrace proposed change.

Make no mistake—all change happens at the level of the individual. When organizations implement small changes as part of a well-crafted strategy, change will be sustainable and more readily accepted than in situations where major change is thrust upon people. No matter how clever your strategy, you must adhere to the principles that you are trying to encourage within your organizational culture and remain open to review and adaptation as you progress along your journey. You must not blindly follow an action plan unless you want to guarantee failure.

Although it is important to know where you are going and to hold on to your vision, you must accept that cultural change takes time. Based on my experience, it takes five to seven years to embed sustainable change within your organization's culture. This time frame does not mean that you must focus all your efforts on it at all times or that meaningful change will not occur along the way. In fact, you will make greater progress if you work through smaller steps.

> **Make no mistake—all change happens at the level of the individual.**

Slow and Steady

Lindsay initially feared that cultural change would be a huge undertaking that would require massive time and resources to achieve. But as she learned about ways people think, interact, and create change within their minds, she understood the lessons of the tortoise: slow and steady can win the race. In some situations, moving slowly will get you to your destination sooner. Small changes do not create resistance in the same way as a major shift. They are easier for people to put into action.

Change can seem easy when we are detached, looking down from above, or thinking about someone else's need for change. If we attempt to change ourselves or our team, many of us will struggle to do so. Think of how hard it can be to give up smoking or start a new exercise program. If you can bear these experiences in mind as you think about organizational change on a global scale, then you will set more realistic expectations for the time it will take.

Most corporate leaders are extremely action oriented. When they make a decision, they are motivated to take immediate action. Not taking action can make them feel ineffective, and even slow action can feel like inaction for them. However, changing mindsets requires patience. It requires a steady, consistent drip of information, actions, feedback, and communication rather than a mission to enforce formal trainings or mandatory guidelines. Least effective but standard in many organizations is a vision that leaders communicate but do not follow or model themselves. Consider instead, *What small action can I take today to support my goals?*

Change does not have to be big to be meaningful.

Change must be intentional. If we know that change begins with the individual, then we know that we must change their neural networks in small, incremental steps. Change must address the core issues; it cannot be "change for the sake of change." Ultimately, leaders must craft the vision with input from all levels, but employees should be the ones who lead the cultural change. Small changes at every level—individual, team, department, and cross-functionally—will advance the larger organism that is the organization. Change does not have to be big to be meaningful. If it is not implemented or sustained, then it is not meaningful at all, irrespective of your shiny PowerPoint slides!

Our Capacity for Change

When you venture to create cultural change, you attempt to rebuild the physical structures of every individual's brain. You seek to convey that your organizational environment is safe and does not harbor judgment, blame, or the risk of dismissal. Instead, this is an environment where people can be themselves and speak out without repercussions. But individual experiences and assumptions are deeply ingrained in the neural structures of the brain. If people have a lifetime of evidence to the contrary, then you will need time to build that trust. You must be consistent in your approach to creating this safer environment, and you will need patience to do it effectively.

One of the most exciting discoveries of the twentieth century was the concept of neuroplasticity.[110] Simply put, the concept suggests that our brains constantly evolve throughout our lives. Every action, thought, and experience changes our brain and develops or reinforces neural pathways within it. Previously, we believed that the brains of adults were "fixed." We thought that our brains developed during childhood, but as we aged, our brain cells died off, contributing to degenerative diseases such as dementia. However, this is not the case. We continuously reproduce brain cells, just as we reproduce cells throughout the rest of our bodies. As we do so, we create and re-create neural pathways and our belief systems. Any changes that you make to yourself, your actions, or your thoughts result in chemical and structural changes to your brain.[111] As a result, we can change our habits, personality, and beliefs. We are not at the whim of our negative thoughts, which tell us that we are powerless to change. Everything can be changed given time and persistence.

Understanding the concept of neuroplasticity clarifies the potential for change within individuals, teams, and culture. We all have capacity for growth and development, but it is rarely an easy journey. We need support for individual growth, opportunities to learn, and a safe environment for experimenting and risk-taking, just as children do when they start to explore the world around them. Perhaps most importantly, we need people and leaders who believe that transformation and growth are possible and who inspire us to commit to taking steps that make way for desired new outcomes. With an understanding of the psychology of change and the neuroscience of our brain's automatic responses, leaders can dramatically improve performance during times of transformation.[112] During these times of rapid change and advancement in the marketplace, we must work toward continual improvement, which underscores the need to shift mindsets from "resistance to change" to "resilience to change." Only then can we stand any chance of success in modern VUCA environments.

Expect to Be Inclusive

When leaders embrace the idea of innovation, they should also be open to new ideas from all avenues rather than having fixed ideas of how to proceed. Employees need to have input in defining their own destinies. They want to feel involved, and they need to exert some level of control. By enabling greater autonomy, leaders can overcome internal resistance toward change. But vision and change are not the sole responsibility of leaders. Their role is to synthesize a clear message out of a broad objective. This message should empower the organization to move as a unified front, but it should also permit complementary visions to be held by departments, teams, and individuals. These symbiotic visions enable employees to feel volition in their own direction while accomplishing goals of the organization. They can believe that their organization's vision coincides with their personal mission and purpose in life. By involving employees in the decision-making process and the journey leaders are taking to define strategy, organizations can overcome the fears that cause resistance to new ideas. Through this collaborative approach, employees feel truly engaged with their work and their lives.

It Is All Too Hard!

Prepare to encounter moments where you feel like giving up. Lindsay certainly experienced this frustration. Usually, her sentiment was a momentary blip, but she doubted her choices a few times when she felt overwhelmed by other pressures and demands from the business. Without structured and consistent support in place, the journey can feel too demanding. When leaders from other business units questioned and criticized her, she doubted herself and her commitment to culture and wondered if she was making the right investment. She wondered, "Are my leaders and I capable? Will it really make a difference?"

If you prepare for these negative thoughts, attitudes, and reactions from other people, but also from yourself, then you will equip yourself to overcome internal resistance. In reality, these feelings of frustration come from your unconscious mind, which is trying to keep you safe. Lindsay's unconscious mind told her, "This is too hard. You might fail and look bad," and "They are going to judge you for this," and "Just do it the way everyone else does it." In those moments, Lindsay had to stop and ask herself, "Is this a real fear, and do I want to limit myself in this manner?" Through this external perspective on her inner thoughts, she actively participated in the decision rather than allowing her unconscious mind to sabotage and keep her in her comfort zone.

Putting It Together

Corporate Synthesis and the creation of culture focus on evolution and development. They reference how we combine the disparate aspects of ourselves or an organization into a coherent whole capable of adaptation. The process begins with insight and awareness, which enable you to take steps toward developing a clear and structured vision. This vision allows for progress and innovation by letting you explore the realms of possibility while remaining firmly grounded in the roots of your individual and organizational reality. When our intent and our actions align with our beliefs and underlying motivations, success becomes achievable for both individuals and entire organizations.

To succeed in cultural change, you need to develop yourself and become a leader who can cultivate a strong team. When you work on yourself, you (and your team) are then more adept in making changes to your organization's culture, which is a living, breathing organism in its own right. This is what will propel you to success.

My intention with this book is not to provide another model for change. As we have discussed, models cannot encompass the complexities and uniqueness of your organization. Instead, I aim to create a safe space for thought. By highlighting some of the processes involved in cultural change, I hope to encourage diversity of thinking around problems occurring within an organization. I also hope to shed light on the variety of possibilities for customizing strategies to propel yourself, your company, and your employees toward greater success.

What follows is an exploration of conditions that can support a business or innovation environment and overcome some of the challenges and resistances that have been highlighted. Later, Part Three delves into the steps that you could take along your journey and the steps that are too often neglected during the rush to implement new ideas and actions. Each step will look and feel different for each leader, team, and organization; however, these steps are conducive to faster and more successful change.

But first, we'll explore why each path is (and should be!) unique.

Summary

- Cultural change is complex and requires us to consider societal and interpersonal issues as well as underlying individual neuropsychology.

- It is better to be proactive than reactive and to develop a culture that enables your organization and employees to adapt to changing circumstances.

- Since change happens at the level of the individual, small steps toward change will create less resistance and foster sustainability in ways that outperform large-scale initiatives.

- It will take time, but the concepts of neuroplasticity show us that change is possible within individuals and systems.

- Successful cultural change is an inclusive process because everyone must engage and commit to the experience.

- You might want to give up during the process, but knowing how your unconscious mind acts as a saboteur will enable you to remain committed to your vision.

- To successfully create a sustainable and innovative culture, you will need to develop yourself as a leader and cultivate a strong team capable of leading a transformation.

6

A Unique Adventure

He who would be a man must therefore be a non-conformist.

—RALPH WALDO EMERSON

By most standards, Lindsay is a successful leader. She is extremely skilled in executing strategy, managing business operations, maintaining financial security, and keeping investors happy. As she climbed the corporate ladder, she received training and mentoring in each of these areas. However, apart from a few basic leadership courses, Lindsay received no training in the skills of emotional intelligence or the psychology of people and organizations. My experience suggests that one of the major barriers to successful cultural change is that business leaders and managers usually know very little about it.

How much training and input did you receive from experts on how to manage people and develop culture?

How much attention have you paid throughout your career to developing your skills in relationships and leadership—the so-called softer skills?

Chances are, not very much compared to your investment in other areas. Even departments that are dedicated to humans focus on them as *resources* rather than as people.

BPT's HR leader, Sarah, focused on ensuring employees gained certain skills and were compensated appropriately and on supporting senior leaders and financial goals of the organization. Like most HR leaders, Sarah was interested in culture and development. However, she acknowledged she had limited understanding of the psychology of individuals and groups and that opportunities to focus on her own knowledge and development were rare. She felt that she was there to manage and corral the people, ensure their basic needs were met, and field any complaints. She also supported other department leaders in handling the inconveniences of human issues whenever they arose. Sarah was overwhelmed by the demands of managing a system that was in place with limited capacity to drive it forward. This gap is common in HR departments, whose budgets are often cut or deprioritized. As such, most organizations offload the issue and call in consultants to undertake the pieces they do not have time or patience to understand. This arrangement is not inherently wrong, but organizations should consider that culture and development initiatives find greater success when trusted people within the organization lead the efforts.

> One of the major barriers to successful cultural change is that business leaders and managers usually know very little about it.

When reflecting on the way that her previous CEO addressed the need for cultural change, Lindsay finally recognized his decision to outsource as a self-protection mechanism. If unsuccessful, he could say, "I paid someone lots of money, and it's not my fault that it didn't work," but if successful, he could take credit for it. When discussing the organization's need for cultural change with her peers, their responses ranged from, "It's not a priority for the business," to "That's HR's role." Peers with a little more understanding admitted, "I know that it's important, but I just don't have the time for this soft stuff." However, what her peers missed, and what Lindsay could now appreciate as a result of this journey and her new knowledge, was that the success of cultural change requires everyone's involvement. Each and every individual within an organization has a role to play, and therefore leadership must come from trusted people within.

Are You Willing to Take on the Challenge?

If you are a leader, then only you can do this. Cultural change will always be more successful when ushered in by a trusted leader within the organization. It will be more palatable and sustainable. As a leader, you must listen to the needs of your organization and tailor the change process to accommodate the unique needs of your people. Involve them in this process rather than handing it off to an outsider who lacks the connection you share with people in your organization.

If you are thinking, "I don't have time for that" or "It's not necessary for *me* to do it," then I invite you to put this book down. If you are unwilling to invest your time in your organization's development, then this book is not for you. On the other hand, if you think that this makes sense, but you have no idea how to start and feel overwhelmed or unequipped, then read on and know that you are not alone in thinking that way.

There is no denying that change at a cultural level is complex. It will take time and effort to implement, but it is done in small increments. With interest and enthusiasm,

You must be willing to learn but also be open to risks and experimentation.

you will have time to lead this change and do your job. You will discover many people who have an interest in these areas and will support you and the changes that you aim to accomplish. In taking a lead in this process, you must confront the discomfort of working outside of your role as an expert and accept the vulnerability of leading changes for which you do not know all the answers. You must be willing to learn but also be open to risks and experimentation. This can be scary, especially when you are a senior leader who feels you must exude confidence and knowledge at all times for people to believe in you—and, perhaps, for you to believe in yourself. Still, this challenge presents great rewards if you are willing to take it on.

Why Should Your Path Be Unique?

Developing culture is a journey of exploring the interconnections between individuals; their ways of thinking, feeling, and behaving; and the disparate parts of your organization. The art of Corporate Synthesis is integrating the many aspects into a coherent whole to achieve clarity. By doing this, we uncover wholeness and bring balance and integrity to all that we do. To achieve a sustainable and positive culture, we must look at ourselves, others, the groups within the organization, and the organization at large. In the same way that no two people are exactly alike, neither are two teams or two organizations within the same industry. Discovering unique ways of working to achieve the right culture for your organization will require understanding the individuality that exists in it at every level.

For Leaders

You are an individual. If you try to copy someone else's style of leadership, the likelihood is that it won't work for you.

As I worked with Lindsay's leadership team, several team members were keen to improve themselves. They had seen the changes and improvements that she had made personally and professionally, and they saw the respect and influence she had garnered and the impact it had had on her career.

A few team members signed up for similar coaching in hopes that following Lindsay's path would afford them the same outcomes. In this case, they were wrong. They were not the same as Lindsay, and they were not beginning with the same motivations. For example, Lindsay was willing to explore not only her strengths but also the dark and ugly sides of her character, and she put in a lot of time and effort to understand and develop those areas. The other team members were not in a place to do that. Some of them wanted a shortcut to success. Others genuinely wanted to learn, but they were unwilling to be vulnerable and dig deep. Still others had not yet developed the requisite self-awareness, and the harder they tried, the more they intellectualized the process. This intellectualization made it harder for them to access their thoughts and feelings and created a roadblock to their development.

Everyone starts in a different place and has to take a different journey. Being willing to explore and understand your personal starting point is vital. We must acknowledge differences in our personalities, challenges we must overcome, and paths we must take to become the best leaders we can possibly be. If we make these efforts, then we can allow ourselves the space and flexibility to develop our unique potential rather than attempting to duplicate a role model. Yes, we can learn from them, but trying to be them rarely works.

> **Everyone starts in a different place and has to take a different journey.**

For Your Team

If we are willing to personalize our path as great leaders, then similarly, we will work differently to develop our teams. A stamp of our personality will exist in whatever we do. We need to be authentic in the way that we lead others, otherwise they will not be inspired to follow and develop good relationships with us.

Teams enable us to reap the benefits of social groups, as we explored in Chapter Three.[113] As each team will have its own outcomes and goals, you need to allow a team to develop in its own way. You may lead three different teams, and each will develop their own "flavor" and unique working style. Although you are the same leader, each team has its own personality. You need to adapt yourself to lead each one effectively and acknowledge the advantages of flexible and situational leadership.

You can effectively adapt your style and lead any team to success if you improve your level of self-awareness and your ability to detect how others respond to you. This will enable you to recognize your team's strengths and weaknesses and strengthen your leadership. The more you can develop these attributes of self-awareness and emotional intelligence in your leaders, the better they will be at creating strength and individuality within your team and other teams to which they belong.

In smaller groups, such as teams within organizations, we are increasingly able to take advantage of our evolutionary predispositions to cooperate for success. Dominance and coercion are common in modern organizations due to hierarchical structures and our perceptions of power. We can maximize the social abilities of groups by releasing these toxic conceptions of leadership. Looking at what motivates people to follow and belong to teams rather than focusing on the role of a leader can teach us how to design effective organizations. Instead of exacerbating the leader dominance models and conformity of team environments, we can lead in ways that meet the needs of every individual. These shifts in mentality lead to innovation and strong cultures that people are committed to sustaining because they can be themselves and adhere to their true values.

For Your Organization

Like with people and teams, each organization is in a different starting place. They have different goals and aspirations, their purposes in the world may vary, and their employees joined them for a wide array of reasons. If you try to apply a standard model to change culture, then you are essentially trying to fit your organization and everyone in it into a neat little box. "But neat boxes and models are so appealing, and everyone likes them," Lindsay said one day. Yes, of course they like them because neat boxes are simple to grasp. But consider how many times you have implemented a simple model for a complex problem and seen it fail.

People are complex because they are subjective rather than objective. A biochemist on one of my psychological safety teams recently complained about the confounding variables that people present. "Wouldn't it be nice if they could all go and live in a lab while we test this stuff out?" he said.

I replied, "Yes. I don't understand why they don't want to do that for years at a time."

People are unique. Even if we could put them in controlled lab conditions as adults, they would still have such wildly differing upbringings, experiences, and beliefs that you could never run an objective experiment. You have to accept that working with people and change falls firmly within a gray area. Leaders and scientists may find this gray area exceedingly difficult to contend with. It can be very frustrating, but to truly understand and make progress, you must be willing to grapple with the uncertainty, complexity, and frustration. The world of psychology can be perplexing. It is not always logical in the ways that data scientists might expect, but there are certainly patterns to identify. For scientists who are willing to examine the evidence, it is there, and it is strong. It simply does not come with the same clarity and strong p-values that scientists anticipate from their lab research data.

In leading a research and discovery organization, Lindsay wanted to separate BPT from the pack in discoveries. She hoped to become the most innovative company in the industry and find the most effective drugs and the most sustainable solutions to some of the world's problems. To accomplish these lofty goals, Lindsay knew that she could not copy the actions of her competitors or companies in other industries. To get my point across to her, I compared this folly of imitation to the notion of copying other companies' models for cultural change. The analogy made Lindsay realize that there was no set path to successful cultural change. The process would involve discovery and innovation, just like all of the organization's other endeavors. Seeing the evidence for developing a unique path based on a realistic understanding of her organization and people helped Lindsay believe that it was a worthwhile investment of her time.

In my experience, successful organizational cultures are typically unique. At KalpTree Energy, every employee is encouraged to make time for fun, which stimulates free thought and creativity and opens the door to developing innovative new technologies.[114] Jeff Bezos insisted that desks at Amazon be constructed from old doors with legs nailed on to serve as a visual illustration of the company philosophy: "We look for every opportunity to save money so we can deliver the best products for the lowest cost."[115] Similarly, Airbnb affirms their business priorities and values in every task, including using meeting rooms designed as living rooms to inspire the relaxed exchange of ideas. This simple emphasis on values led to a reduction in the need for corporate processes.[116]

To encourage cooperation and innovation in the pharmaceutical world, Eli Lilly celebrates research failures to publicly recognize hard work and the reality that failure is a huge part of success in innovation. Elanco Animal Health employees nominate each other for awards such as the Golden Tree, highlighting a commitment to speaking candidly and promoting psychological safety, and the Golden Plunger for doing the dirty work that no one wanted to do, while Roivant Sciences developed a program to reward employees for raising red flags about research that may need to be halted.[117] Sometimes from the outside, people question the need for these practices that elucidate the culture, but creating concepts and practices that feel distinctive and compelling to those inside the organization can contribute to strong and cohesive cultures.[118]

As every organization is unique, solutions must be unique and customized for each environment. As a leader, you hold much expertise about your company, the way it functions, and its existing culture. If you are willing to step back and look at it with fresh eyes, then you will discover more than you could imagine about where you are now and the possibilities for future directions.

To build an organization that can be successful in the marketplace, attract and retain talent, and most importantly, sustain a culture that allows that talent to be optimized and released from the typical organizational and individual subconscious restraints, you must be brave enough to step out of normal patterns, create something unique, and enable yourself and your organization to stand out in the world. As innovator Bill Taylor so neatly says, "If you are doing things at your company that outsiders can't quite understand, then you may just be doing it right."[119]

Why You Need to Lead

Although Lindsay had a great deal of experience with large consultancies running cultural change processes at her previous organizations, she had never had the opportunity to be directly involved. As she reflected on her work with consultancies, she acknowledged, "It seemed easy, but we never liked the result."

I hear this quite often from executives.

I also hear things like, "It doesn't quite seem to fit" or "It was great for six months, but inevitably it collapses or isn't quite the same when they leave."

It takes courage to forge a new path and do something innovative.

To be clear, I am talking about cultural change here; I'm not commenting on other processes or strategic changes. These opinions are driven by the simple fact that these executives had no real ownership of the change because someone else ran it for them, and the organization and employees did not feel included or heard. This brings us back to the neurological resistance to change and its impact on sustainable change. If we look outside for change because we doubt our ability to achieve it or because it seems less risky to our career and position, then we do not take ownership or truly commit to supporting the culture or the needs of our employees. It takes courage to forge a new path and do something innovative.

Coordinate Your Efforts

One of the biggest mistakes I see organizations make in managing the people aspects of the business is not coordinating their efforts. They tackle culture at an organizational level, professional development at an individual level, and performance at a process level. They separate coaching, learning, and innovation instead of approaching them as interdependent and integral parts of the whole. They confuse purpose and engagement with culture rather than viewing them as pieces of a larger puzzle.

> **As a leader, you have knowledge of and influence in your organization. Use it!**

To successfully improve and develop a positive culture that supports both people and organizational goals, it is essential that all efforts are coordinated across the organization to achieve Corporate Synthesis. Employees should see a cohesive and thoughtful plan in action rather than a mishmash of reactionary interventions. If done well, this leads to a perception of continuous improvement instead of constant change and reinvention, which only sets up resistance to new ideas. It is vital to bring together the disparate parts of the organization to understand it as a whole organism that needs to function in unison.

As a leader, you have knowledge of and influence in your organization. Use it! Corporate Synthesis is about uncovering the interconnections that exist within all systems at all levels. It is about uncovering the challenging aspects that are present and seeing what they can contribute to the situation. Our weaknesses as well as our strengths play a part in enabling us to move forward to success. Examining where we are and where we want to be allows us the opportunity to rediscover aspects of our identity that have been excluded from our lives or workplaces and turn weakness into strength.

To learn or to take action, we sometimes need to separate ideas and concepts into their component parts. Doing this without understanding the complexity of the whole system tends to leave us wondering where it went wrong or causes us to throw the baby out with the bathwater because we tried to implement the ideas in isolation. Looking at the whole can help you develop your unique path to successful cultural change.

Summary

- A major obstacle to cultural change is a lack of knowledge about how to do it.

- To find success in this endeavor, you must take the time to learn and understand how to change culture and be willing to lead the transformation yourself.

- It is important to acknowledge that as a leader, you are unique, your team is unique, and your organization is unique.

- To stand out in the world, you must have the courage to follow your own path and develop the culture that is effective for your organization.

- People want to follow leaders they trust, those who have knowledge and experience in the organization, and those who care about their people. This is your role.

- To tame the culture tiger, you must coordinate your efforts across the organization and recognize that culture is part of everything you do.

7

Envisioning a New Environment

Once you have an innovation culture, even those who are not scientists or engineers...embrace the meaning of what it is to be scientifically literate. They embrace the concept of an innovation culture.

—NEIL DEGRASSE TYSON

"Where do you want your organization to be in five years?" I asked Lindsay.

"I want us to be the leader of our industry—unquestionably the most innovative biopharmaceutical across our entire range of products and delivery systems," she responded. "Our culture can give us a competitive advantage and support us in achieving complex, innovative work while lowering costs to the business and reducing time for approval and getting products to market."

"Okay, but what does that look like on a day-to-day basis at the differing levels of the organization?" I asked.

Lindsay had a clear vision. "At an individual level, we would see employees engaged with their work and achieving their goals. They would be curious and motivated to explore new ideas and concepts and keen to engage and collaborate with other equally enthusiastic colleagues. They would have autonomy to make their own decisions and take their personal development in the direction of their own choosing, as well as focusing on learning leadership skills to promote their careers. I think there would be a sense of optimism, and people would be happy and productive in their work," she said.

"I hope that people would have a sense of well-being, that their stress levels would be low and their health good because we know that stress interferes with people's cognitive capacity and achievement potential," she continued. "Employee well-being would benefit not only individuals and their ability to achieve work-life integration but also the organization, because resilient employees are more able to adapt and respond to the continual flux we face in meeting the demands of our industry."

Lindsay wasn't finished. "At a business level, employee well-being would translate to reduced attrition and increased motivation to achieve outcomes. It would save money through sustained productivity but also in recruitment, healthcare, and absentee costs. We would increase the speed to market of products and the efficiency of operations.

"Trusting relationships between colleagues, both within teams and cross-functionally, would lead to greater sharing of information internally, increase collaboration and problem-solving, and encourage diversity of thinking and creativity—all of which are essential for innovation. A willingness to take risks as individuals and as teams and to view failure as an opportunity to learn rather than a personal deficiency or a catastrophe would inspire an environment in which we could all be continually learning and improving. This psychologically safe environment would catapult us toward our goals rather than hold us back out of fear of negative consequences.

And finally, "Our leaders would pioneer the way with their actions and behaviors by focusing on emotional intelligence, being vulnerable, and willing to admit their own failings and uncertainties. We would see leaders promoting the cultural ideals at all levels of the organization, ensuring accountability for the behaviors that we value, and maintaining high standards in all of our work. These attributes would help us overcome the challenges that we face, including our individual fears and concerns, the anxiety we can feel about our status and expertise in the hierarchy, geographical boundaries, the challenges of being a global company, and working virtually across different cultures."

She ended with, "I guess that's quite a big wish list!"

What Is Required for Innovation?

As we develop cultures of innovation and aim to achieve wish lists like Lindsay's to create sustainable practices, we need to consider that we might want more than new solutions or ideas but instead, a system and mindset that allows us to ask better questions and gain a deeper understanding of our current context. We all know that as things evolve, yesterday's solutions often become today's problems, especially when those solutions were set into motion but never reviewed, revised, or adapted to the current needs of the organization. What worked five years ago is unlikely to remain the solution today unless it evolved with the changing needs of the world around it.

> **As things evolve, yesterday's solutions often become today's problems.**

To innovate, change, and move forward, we need to be adaptable. People need to be in an environment that enables this and allows each individual to be agile in their mindset and interactions. We need to understand how each person operates within the system, both practically and psychologically, and what will enable them to develop the capabilities to become more agile.

How Can We Create an Innovation Environment?

Imagine being the parent of a two-year-old child.

Many of you reading this have had this experience or have witnessed your friends and family in these circumstances. At some point in the distant past, you were that two-year-old. As a parent, you expect certain behavior from your child. You hope they will perform well, sit nicely in the restaurant, and happily accompany you on your trip to the store. But do these hopes play out in reality? How often are you dragging an unwilling child behind you, hushing them at the table so that they do not disturb other diners, or worst of all, looking on helplessly as the child flings itself to the ground in a tantrum, wailing and screaming that "everything is all your fault" and "life is so unfair"?

When you think about creating or changing culture, you must think about your goals as a leader, the goals for your organization, the role that other people play in getting you there, and the environment that can support them. You also need to consider how to create and achieve this vision without setting off internal resistances that can prevent it.

As a parent or future parent, you have probably spent time thinking about how you would raise your children. The ways in which you would encourage good behavior and positive attributes. If you don't have children, then you may have even stronger views on what parents should be doing!

We all know at some level that the key to raising kids is having clear structures, boundaries, and consistency within the environment around them, partnered with their freedom to explore the world and develop their individuality. This is not an easy pairing, and is definitely easier said than done! We follow all the parenting advice to create an environment to raise good humans by instilling naughty steps, keeping rewards charts, and setting expectations and rules.[120] Still, there is always a fear that too much rigidity will stifle the little darlings from developing their creativity, their individuality, or (in the case of *your* child, of course) their genius. Herein lies the difficulty. *How do you strike a balance between structure and freedom or between expected outcomes and individuality?*

In companies, we seek balance between structure, rules, and hierarchy on the one hand and risk-taking, creativity, and innovation on the other. It's between having freedom and psychological safety, accountability and control. This struggle to satisfy competing interests is an experience that parents and organizations share. If we view a leader in a role similar to a parent, then their will, personality, and personal belief system around "the way things should be done" often determines the balance within the company.

Although circumstances and contexts change throughout our lives, our basic needs for certainty and belonging remain.

An authoritarian leader naturally leans toward structure and rigidity, wanting people to perform in a prescribed manner, to accomplish their will. These tendencies lead to micromanagement and the belief that they can better perform everyone's jobs. Like the parents in the playground constantly calling out instructions and safety guidance, these leaders hover over their employees, determining what they will do and achieve. This behavior limits the ability of people to achieve at their optimum because there is no space for freedom of thought or creativity.

At the opposite end of the spectrum, we have the leader who only ever thinks about innovation. For them, the workplace is a playground with all the fun things that were popular as perks a few years ago, on the assumption that they would stimulate creativity and bonding. If it is such a fun place to work, then why would anyone leave? But like the child who has complete freedom, we find an underlying anxiety and a need for guidance. "What am I doing here?" wonder our employees. With no boundaries, our two-year-old runs amok in a desperate bid for attention, or they withdraw quietly into a corner, fearful of other children and adults.

Although circumstances and contexts change throughout our lives, our basic needs for certainty and belonging remain. Our employees reflect this when they feel anxiety about what they are doing and where they fit in and when they feel a need for security and accomplishment. With little or no guidance from above—or conversely, too much control—they feel insecure. "Am I achieving? What is my purpose? How will it reflect on me? Am I safe? Do I belong?" When you think about culture, you must think about both the environment in which people operate and their individual motivations, mindsets, and need to belong to social groups.

Environments That Support Innovation

When trying to understand what made teams effective, Harvard researcher Amy Edmondson discovered that teams performing highly on measures of team effectiveness appeared to be making more errors than the lower-performing teams.[121] This research, supported by further studies, made a strong case for the idea that variations in the interpersonal climate within teams were leading to a reporting bias and this counterintuitive result.

As we explored in Part One, as humans we are often fearful of taking risks and failing due to our underlying beliefs about the world and our needs to belong, maintain our self-esteem, and manage the impressions of others. If we are spending our time and mental energy worrying what others think, then we are less likely to be engaged with our tasks or creative processes. We are also less likely to take risks, which is a major barrier to innovation. *What, then, did these high-performing teams have that enabled them to overcome their innate thinking and fears in order to be willing to fail, take risks, and learn?*

Google asked a similar question when it launched Project Aristotle in 2012 to find out what attributes make a team effective at Google. A global study on 180 teams, with double-blind interviews and data from existing surveys examining over 250 team attributes and including psychological safety as a variable, found that an individual's perception of consequences for taking an interpersonal risk on a team was the most important factor that impacted team effectiveness.[122] In other words, the difference between high- and low-performing teams was *how* they worked together rather than *who* was on the team.[123] This conclusion offered additional support for Edmondson's findings and her concept of psychological safety.

What Is Psychological Safety?

At its core, psychological safety is a shared belief that a group environment is safe for interpersonal risk-taking.[124] When people have a sense of being accepted and respected, they can recognize that others value their contributions. These sentiments create a safe place for employees to share new ideas without the lurking, or real, fear that there will be negative consequences or judgments that affect their career, reputation, or self-image.

When Mike spoke up with an innovative idea in Chapter Two, Lindsay dismissed it. In doing so, she left Mike feeling anxious. Perhaps his idea was foolish or not good enough. Did everyone think that he didn't know what he was talking about? Had he lost Lindsay's respect by speaking up? This situation triggered his internal beliefs and fears and caused a stress response, but it also altered his future behavior, beliefs about the team environment, and perceptions of his colleagues' attitudes toward him.

If Lindsay's response had been different, how might Mike have felt? By welcoming the idea and being open to exploring it, regardless of the eventual outcome, Lindsay could have created greater psychological safety not just for Mike but for the whole team. The team would have witnessed an invitation to be curious and share and a clear example of safe risk-taking. For an organization where innovation is key, where it is critical for people to feel empowered to share ideas and think creatively, a sense of belonging and psychological safety are essential for optimum success.

Is Psychological Safety the Whole Story?

No, I am afraid that it is not that simple. Psychological safety is a foundational stone. It is one part of culture that enhances the efforts you make in other areas of the business. Psychological safety does not, in and of itself, create effective or productive interpersonal collaboration because it is merely a first step, without which collaboration is limited.[125] Psychological safety exists on a continuum and as such already exists to some extent in your workplace. Your role is to enhance it and recognize that the degree of psychological safety will vary in different teams and departments and that each of them will have a unique journey to improvement. There is no one-size-fits-all approach.

The good news is that psychological safety can serve as a foundation to almost any culture as long as you value the attributes of inclusiveness, engagement, and involvement at every level of an organization and are willing to take that commitment seriously. Psychological safety is a group-level construct and not an individual one.[126] For example, at BPT, Sam (who we met in Chapter Four) felt very safe saying whatever he wanted to his team and considered himself psychologically safe; however, his behavior created frustration and unease in other team members, who felt criticized or undermined by him. Because of this, the team as a whole was not psychologically safe. This example shows how individual and group experiences of safety are symbiotic. The strengths of a team and its level of psychological safety comes from its individual members, and the strength of individual members is enhanced by the strengths and psychological safety within the team. It is hard to create sustainable health in one without the other, and at a broader level, the same applies to culture and the whole organization.

Systemic and Individual Resilience

Teams are made up of people. If we want high-performing, effective teams and organizations, then we need to think about the individuals who comprise them. As we learned in Part One, most resistance to new ideas comes from individuals, and most business and scientific success also stems from individuals. We know that people do not function optimally if they are stressed, afraid, or feel excluded from groups, so we have to ensure that we meet their needs if we want to get the best from them. Ideally, like Lindsay, we want our employees to be resilient, adaptable, and willing to respond to change with open minds. We also want to ensure that we are meeting their desires for personal development and understanding their motivations.

Why do people respond differently to similar events, and why are some people more resilient than others?

Essentially, resiliency is the ability to bounce back from failure and setbacks or to overcome adversity. The question then becomes, *Why do people respond differently to similar events, and why are some people more resilient than others?* Researchers have rigorously examined this trait during childhood to understand why some people overcome trauma and develop resilience and others fail to do so.

An interesting longitudinal study begun in 1955 in Kauai followed children born into hardship and found that only a third of the children thrived in the face of adversity during childhood, suggesting low rates of resiliency.[127] However, for us, thinking about workplace resilience, more noteworthy was that most of the other two-thirds had turned their lives around and developed resilience by age forty. This demonstrated that resilience is not a fixed or inherent trait but something that people can develop throughout their lives. If we want resilient employees within organizations, then we need to think about how we support their development and how the environment they work in may improve or erode their resiliency. Resiliency is getting more attention in the workplace these days. Unfortunately, it is often represented as an individual's responsibility to overcome stress or challenges. Their struggle in this area is taken as a sign of weakness. For Ben, the change leader at BPT we met at the start of Chapter Three, we saw how constantly combating opposition and resistance to his ideas ultimately wore him down. Over time, his resilience dwindled, and he chose to acquiesce to the dominant ideas and culture rather than move forward with his novel ideas. In the end, Ben's environment greatly impacted his resiliency.

Kirsty found that moving into a team with a supportive manager and peers within a psychologically safe organization enabled her to become increasingly resilient. She could respond more effectively to failures in her lab without blaming herself or worrying about consequences to her career. Although Kirsty's environment helped improve her resiliency, so did the people around her.

If we think about Corporate Synthesis and the interconnections between individuals, groups, and societies, it becomes clear that we need to look at resilience from a systemic perspective. Individual resilience utilizes resources from many other systems.[128] Some come from within, such as our abilities to problem solve, regulate our emotions, and self-motivate, while others are developed from external factors, such as our experiences of the world, childhood attachments, and the social and cultural beliefs that we internalize. Some are biological, such as our personal responses to stress, and others are situational and dependent on our environments, the people around us and how we experience them.[129] It is important to realize that all of these elements are in dynamic relationships with one another. Our levels of resilience can change over time, depending on our strengths and experiences in each of these areas.

When Kirsty was resilient, she found that she could better handle stress and change. When stress became chronic or her environment was unsupportive, her resiliency diminished. This is vital for organizations and leaders to understand because if, as individuals, we are resilient, we are better able to contribute to a psychologically safe team and build positive, trusting relationships. We are less likely to succumb to stress and all the negative impacts that entails. However, we must look at it systemically from all sides because if our teams are psychologically safe, then we have a greater ability to become resilient—both as teams and as individuals.[130] None of these dynamics are one way or exist in isolation.

To create healthy cultures, organizations have a responsibility to reduce stress in the workplace, support employees in developing healthy emotional management and stress responses, and change working practices and procedures to enable these changes. We need to think about how culture reflects the whole person inside and outside of work and how to set and model our expectations of employees. Statements around well-being mean nothing without action to make it reality, and that only occurs when the concern for people's well-being is genuine.

We will be well on our way to creating the foundations for a successful business if we can support the development of individual resilience in team members and help them to overcome their internal limitations while creating beneficial environments at the team and organizational levels. Under these conditions, people can thrive and achieve the strategic vision and scientific discoveries that spell success.

Relationships Matter

Lindsay had observed within her leadership team that some leaders attained greater results than others. Those who prioritized their people and connection seemed to have greater followings. They enjoyed less conflict and resolved issues more easily. One of her directors, Carlos, had consistently high engagement scores within his department. In most departments, turnover of people and teams reflected employee requests to move within or totally leave the organization. Although turnover in Carlos's department was comparable to others, the reason was very different. Carlos's team members were seen as valuable resources and were relocated within the organization for the impact they could have.

Cognizant that statistics never tell the whole story, Lindsay observed Carlos more closely. She noticed Carlos's genuine investment of time in his employees and his level of emotional intelligence while doing so. The positive feelings Carlos fostered in others garnered greater support for his ideas, more open communication, and closer cooperation between his teams. The creativity and engagement that Lindsay observed contrasted with what she witnessed in clinical operations with Sam's more authoritarian leadership. Lindsay came to understand that authentic leaders can leverage social behaviors that reinforce our brain's social systems. As Carlos demonstrated, this is more successful in developing teams, encouraging cooperation, and enhancing the organization's ability to innovate and lead in the market. Lindsay considered why some people appeared to have this ability while others did not and thought about where she might fall on this continuum as well as what impact she might be having on her employees.

So much stress is created by poor relationships. We all know the adage, "People don't leave jobs; they leave managers." The truth of this is reflected in the statistic that over 50 percent of Americans have left a job to get away from a manager during their careers.[131] But it is not just managers; it is how we get along with colleagues and how we feel treated by the organization as a whole. *Do we feel we fit in and have a purpose? Are we valuable, and do we make a contribution?* All of these things affect how we feel, and most of those feelings come from the quality of our interactions with those around us and the way we feel they perceive us. It is our need to belong coming into play.

The environment around us can create or reduce stress. It is important that we get it right for our employees and for ourselves so we can function at our optimum and allow our brains to reach their potential. This is how we succeed as individuals, as teams, as organizations, and as innovators.

Developing Others

You probably have a host of technically proficient experts within your organization. For a scientific endeavor, this is critical. But many of these experts were not trained as leaders. Reflecting on her first job in a lab, Lindsay recalled how one of her colleagues, Rani, had been promoted to supervisor. Rani was the strongest individual contributor on the team, but no one had considered whether she had the skills to lead, and she received no training in managing or developing others. Looking back, Lindsay could see how that promotion set Rani up to fail. When she did not meet expectations as a manager, Rani was demoted. This chain of events diminished her sense of self-worth and damaged her relationships with her managers and the organization. It destroyed any sense of psychological safety that Rani had and made her doubt her value to the organization. Since others knew what had happened to her and she shared her story with some, like Lindsay, this added to the cultural story of risk, blame, and pejorative consequences in the organization: "If it could happen to her, it could happen to me."

If we gave thought to leadership development earlier in careers, we could avoid many of these issues. To develop leaders capable of leading change and growth in the modern economy, organizations need to facilitate whole-person growth by supporting people to develop personally as well as professionally. If we think about the social and evolutionary roles of leaders as situational and temporary, then the importance of modeling and developing leadership skills at every level of an organization becomes apparent.

By doing this, creating a greater sense of self-awareness, and fostering the attributes of emotional intelligence, we support people in becoming more resilient and enable them to adapt and support others in changing circumstances.

Organizations need to facilitate whole-person growth by supporting people to develop personally as well as professionally.

A leader only becomes better by focusing on their own internal improvement first because this gives them greater insight into supporting the development of others. Rather than sending people on two-day leadership trainings, we need to make this development part of the culture. Then people can learn these skills and attributes early, alongside an understanding of the underlying principles of culture, the importance of humans and how their subjective views and experiences are relevant to the way an organization functions. If this knowledge is endemic, then you make it easier for new hires as well as old hands to adopt and learn these attitudes and skills through their daily interactions with others.

When I look at organizations that take the time to ensure these cultural ideals permeate every level of the organization, I usually see the most junior employees become interested. They want to develop and learn; they want to understand these ideas and implement them—and why wouldn't they? On the lowest rungs of the organization, culture impacts them, but they have the least control over their day-to-day experience. Offering them knowledge allows them to instill this thinking in their daily work lives, and it gives them the chance to take action and disseminate this knowledge as they climb the corporate ladder.

What I know, and Lindsay quickly discovered, was that as this knowledge permeates your organization, you will discover that you have natural leaders and managers who are capable of developing others and holding them accountable. Succession management issues reduce as a result. Emerging leaders have a greater ability to create psychologically safe teams and positive cultures of well-being. This leadership development becomes self-perpetuating and sustainable. As people understand and experience the benefits the new culture brings, they will choose to be engaged, and positive cultural attributes will weather changes and support your organizational goals over the years. With reduced attrition and an engaged workforce, you will likely become a sought-after employer with your pick of talent because people want "to do what they do best," and they will choose to work in an environment with leaders who enable this.[132] To have successful cultures that support innovative work, we need to ensure that our managers and leaders are equipped to create environments that facilitate employees to develop and understand the concepts relevant to culture, change, and well-being.

People Want Purpose

Purpose is often touted as a priority for employee engagement, and it is certainly an important factor that brings both meaning and a sense of security to people. At several companies with which I work, they promote the corporate purpose volubly. In the life science arena, where I often find myself, employees feel a great sense of purpose because scientists make discoveries that have the potential to change lives. These scientists know that they contribute to changing the world's landscape in terms of food security, health, and environmental safety. Leaders have a big role to play in communicating this purpose and creating a shared meaning for teams and organizations.

However, it's important to understand that the corporate purpose may not be the same as individual purpose and that there is a risk that purpose and passion can lead to burnout. Phillipe worried that if he was not seen to be working long hours or dared to take a vacation, then his commitment to the organization's purpose would be questioned. Sigrid was excited and thrilled by the science that she explored every day, but like many others, her dedication and passion for her work reduced her work-life balance and increased her stress, which led to exhaustion, cynicism, and burnout.[133] Corporate purpose can have a dark side, and even when used effectively, it is just one factor of many that contribute to engagement. Purpose is not your culture. If it is the only area into which you put your time and effort, assuming that employees are only motivated by the bigger picture of their contributions, then you are laboring under a major misconception.

Purpose is not your culture.

People are primarily engaged and motivated by the quality of interpersonal collaboration within their workplace and the meaning, or individual purpose, they derive from it.[134] If you want high levels of engagement and collaboration, then you need to create a foundation of psychological safety, resilience, and open, honest communication that promotes trust and respect. Your chosen culture sits upon this foundation. It is an essential building block to whatever you create, and purpose can be part of a structure that sits on top of it.

Are We Achieving Anything?

I often get the question, "If we are all being so nice to each other, then how will we achieve goals or get any real work done?" It's a fair question. Let's look at three teams within BPT to explore this further.

Carrie, a biochemistry lead for vaccines, had worked hard to create a high level of psychological safety in her team, and members willingly shared their ideas, but there was very little accountability. The result was limited productivity and reduced performance standards. Team members were rarely pushed out of their comfort zones, and without the need to stretch themselves, innovation rarely occurred.

The majority of teams with which I work are more like Simon's in medical diagnostics and have the opposite issue to Carrie's. Both Simon, as the team leader, and the organization applied pressure and high levels of accountability to team members, but there was little psychological safety. Simon's team members felt concerned that they may shoulder the blame for mistakes, so they were unwilling to speak up due to fear and anxiety. This lack of psychological safety meant errors went unidentified and product quality was reduced. In one situation, this led to patient harm and a subsequent lawsuit. Research projects were prolonged at significant financial cost because the team did not want to look like they were failing.

Mary's team in vaccine development had little accountability or psychological safety, and she struggled to engage or motivate her team. No one would speak up because without psychological safety, they were unwilling to be vulnerable or take a risk when they doubted a positive outcome. As a result, innovation was limited.

Ideally, to achieve high standards of work, a team should have high levels of both psychological safety and accountability. These attributes position them perfectly for learning and innovation, as we see in the following diagram.[135]

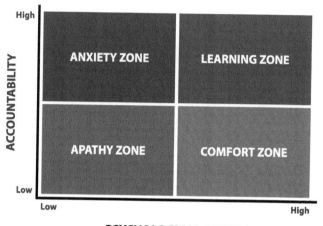

In reality, no team remains in any one of these zones constantly. Our attitudes toward projects and colleagues often shift, and typically, I find that an organization moves through all of these zones. You can even flow through each of these differing conditions during a single meeting. The key is to recognize where you are in each moment and what is lacking and then take steps to move the group back to the conditions that support learning and growth. Shuntaro did this when he recognized that conflict around deadlines was pushing his team toward anxiety and readjusted his strategies to find out how everyone was feeling, enabling them to work together to achieve their goals and return to a learning mindset. When Jasmine noticed her team was becoming complacent and not asking questions that supported diversity, she guided them back into the learning zone, encouraging a curious mindset to ensure they were not missing opportunities.

Accountability is important in so many ways as we create psychologically safe cultures. However, it is important to remember that accountability does not mean being harsh or punitive, although sadly, it is taken this way by many organizations. Rather, it describes a willingness to accept responsibility for one's own actions or to encourage another to do the same.[136] For individuals, teams, and whole organizations, this willingness can empower us to make successful and sustainable changes in the way we behave at all levels. As you start to develop new ideals in culture, it is vital that you hold yourself and others accountable to these new behaviors.

Most leaders and managers are uncomfortable holding people accountable, especially for behaviors as opposed to deadlines and procedures, which may appear to be more black and white. It is important to understand this discomfort and know that for most people, it stems from their internal fear of how others see them and their desire to remain part of the group. Leading by example is crucial here. It is critical that you are not asking others to do something that they are not comfortable or skilled in doing or that you or your leadership team are not able to do yourselves. If you want innovation, and I'm assuming if you lead an R&D organization you do, then you must be willing to thoughtfully create an environment that enables it by effectively modeling the behaviors that will make it sustainable.

Pay Attention to Processes, Procedures, and Systems

Processes and procedures are your operating standards and how you get things done, along with the way that your organization is structured. They have a huge impact on how people experience work. They cause major frustration and stress for many people and are often ignored in discussions about culture and personal development, but the two are intrinsically linked. Although this book and my work as a psychologist focuses on the human aspects of culture, ignoring the impact of day-to-day operations on employees' ability to do their jobs would be a grave error.

The details and practical implementation can vary so wildly between organizations that dwelling on it here would not be a good use of time. However, one thing I have discovered from many years of experience is that if you have created an environment where everyone can speak up about issues and share ideas without worrying how they will be perceived, then you will get so much information about what limits the organization. You will hear how processes can be improved and what truly motivates people. You will discover that many of these dilemmas and frustrations can be resolved much more easily than you could have imagined and that systematizing basic processes can free employees to be increasingly creative—although in scientific environments, we must take care not to systematize so far that we kill the ability to innovate.

Everyone must feel empowered to contribute.

For this to be effective, everyone must feel empowered to contribute. Those with the authority to act must listen and make change where it seems optimal to do so. This sounds simple, but I have rarely seen an organization where it is commonplace. When you view your employees as the experts, then you can empower them to make the decisions that truly matter to them rather than imposing your own perceived solutions from on high. The key is to think about the impact it has on the way people function, operate, think, and feel in their environment and to consider what resistances or fears you might be activating within them through your actions or decisions.

Communication is key. It must be transparent, clear, and honest to keep people engaged and to build trusting relationships. This is as true for corporate communications as it is for one-to-one relationships and conversation. Giving and receiving honest and constructive feedback is essential between all layers of an organization because this is how people and organizations learn and grow. It is better to admit what you do not know than to fabricate an explanation or reassure people, and by modeling this, you build trust and give your team the confidence to adopt this approach as well. The reasons that leaders so often fail to do this tie back to our human needs to protect ourselves, to be liked, and to remain part of the group. Leaders may also fail to trust other people or feel fearful of their reactions to their uncertainty.

These practical elements of organization—from policies to communications, strategies, and hierarchies—need to reflect the culture consistently and accurately. Be clear about how they align and evolve with business goals and how culture is relevant to the daily work employees do.

Culture is not separate from your business and work; it is woven through the very fabric of everything each person does every day.

Putting It Together

Let us revisit Maslow's hierarchy of needs, introduced in Part One, which posits that people first work to meet their physiological needs, then their safety, followed by love and belonging, then self-esteem, and then, finally—if all of these are met—they can think about self-actualization and their desire to achieve their potential.[137] When you consider the concepts we have discussed in this chapter in terms of Maslow's hierarchy of needs, you can see why the creation of the environment is crucial to the development of an innovation culture. Knowing that an individual cannot move from one level of the hierarchy until their previous needs have been fulfilled, we can see how important it is for organizations to address individual and group needs.

> **Culture is not separate from your business and work; it is woven through the very fabric of everything each person does every day.**

For most employees, their physiological needs in the hierarchy are met. However, even these can be compromised by undue stress, so we must work to reduce that. Feeling secure in their employment for financial stability and to provide for themselves and their families is vital. The foundation created by a psychologically safe workplace addresses these needs by removing the fears and insecurities about not belonging, feeling judged, and losing their job and security, which is an underlying fear for many who worry about speaking up or sharing ideas that might not be universally accepted.

It is vital that leaders have, and use, their knowledge of the human condition to create teams and provide support to individuals. It is equally important that they understand the contribution of culture and the workplace environment as they endeavor to create supportive and accepting relationships throughout the organization.

We know that people are working hard consciously and unconsciously to protect their self-image and their self-esteem, but it is only when they feel confident in their environment that they can truly begin to feel that they are worthy. When they feel respected, they can begin to appreciate their own accomplishments. We can enhance this by recognizing their good work, praising rather than only criticizing them, giving them the experience of seeing accountability to expected behaviors, and enabling them to release some of the anxiety around how they are judged so they can become more resilient.

With this environment in place, people become free to explore their own potential, and their brains are released from evolutionary constraints and the impact of the stress response. Now they can function efficiently and utilize all of its cognitive capabilities. In reaching this state, people can follow their drive to achieve, learn, develop, and join with others in pursuit of a purpose, where they can become creative and willing to take risks, fail, and succeed, both individually and within teams.

If we think back to the development of a child, the simplicity is apparent. As young children, we are (hopefully) in a safe environment where our basic needs are met. Our caregivers love us and protect us from danger, providing a refuge where we can return after we explore the world and interact with peers. We are encouraged and given boundaries, and we learn what to expect from our environment and those within it. At the same time, we are protected from bullies and discrimination. With these circumstances in place as we develop, we are free to explore our own interests, be creative, learn new things, solve problems, and follow our desires.

If adults fail to provide children with these conditions, then we have hungry children who cannot concentrate in school. These children experience separation anxiety or uncertainty about engaging in new activities, so they are limited in their exploration of the world. Without a sense of belonging, children may struggle to make friends and withdraw from family. If their self-esteem is low, they will not be independent or think well of themselves, which will cause them to doubt and limit themselves. While it is simpler to see in an individual child's development, the same is true of our minds and needs as adults—the complexities just seem greater and are less visible than they are in the simplicity of childhood.

As a leader of an organization, you can create the conditions for your people to thrive, just as caregivers create the circumstances for children to thrive.

At every level, corporate and cultural synthesis, organizational development, and success are about the integration of individuals and groups. It is about how people think and function within their minds and how they come together in relationship with each other. We must constantly inquire about what motivates and limits them in order to understand how we can best support them, understand their motivations, and how we can align ourselves and our goals to fit with those needs. It is a true synthesis of minds, people, development, teams, and goals.

Summary

- Innovation is a mindset—a way of thinking and behaving that enables diversity, a willingness to take risks and collaborate on ideas.

- Modern corporate environments tend to create anxiety and uncertainty, which impacts our higher cognitive functioning and our ability to innovate.

- To overcome our evolutionary and unconscious fears in order to innovate, we need to be in a psychologically safe environment.

- To be cognitively flexible and able to cope with change, both individuals and organizations need to be resilient.

- We must focus on the development, engagement, and well-being of individuals because they will ultimately determine an organization's culture.

- Psychological safety, accountability, resilience, and well-being are important, but we must also consider the impact of our communications, structures, processes, and procedures on how people engage with cultural change.

- As a leader, you are responsible for creating the environment that enables your employees to be innovative.

PART THREE

PREPARING FOR CULTURAL CHANGE

8 | Becoming a Trusted Leader— It Starts with You

Yesterday I was clever, so I wanted to change the world.
Today I am wise, so I am changing myself.

—RUMI

As a senior leader, Lindsay had a wide sphere of influence that went far beyond her abilities to strategize and create policy. Not only did she directly impact the success of the organization and the decisions that were taken, but she also impacted the experience of each person working within it. A lack of self-awareness or an inability to regulate her emotions and interactions would have had a direct and negative impact on trust, well-being, and the overall culture. Lindsay could see how this affected productivity, efficiency, and quality of decision-making, as well as the ability of the organization to innovate. Her behavior determined the loyalty of her employees and set the tone for how they behaved and what they felt empowered to bring to the workplace.

A leader is the steward of the culture, and as Lindsay recognized, if you want the culture to change, you must become the architect of the vision and exemplify what you wish to develop. For people to follow you, they need to trust in your authenticity and ability to lead. Our social nature means we want to follow leaders we see as influential within a group. We want to be liked and respected by them since their influence can determine whether we remain part of that group—and in the workplace, it affects our career. Being socially motivated, we attempt to emulate the behavior and habits of those whom we see as successful because we desire the same outcomes.

A leader is the steward of the culture.

As a leader, consider the ways that you are perceived as having power, prestige, and status, and know that if you are seen as successful, then people will want to emulate you. Therefore, you have a unique opportunity to influence and guide culture, through the behavior you model, as well as the words you say. You probably have some work to do, because none of us are perfect and there is always room for improvement. When people see your willingness to change yourself, they will be inspired to follow suit or at least consider the possibility that change is not all bad—but everything starts with you.

In this chapter, we will discuss how you can inspire more trust in your leadership by learning to be more self-aware, practicing empathy in relationships, understanding perceptions (internally and externally), and being more vulnerable.

Becoming Self-Aware

Until you make the unconscious conscious,
it will direct your life and you will call it fate.
—C. G. JUNG

Becoming self-aware is a vital first step in developing emotional intelligence.[138] Without self-awareness, you cannot make progress in sustainable change, whether personal or organizational. It is one of the hallmarks of a great leader. It demonstrates a capacity to honestly evaluate your actions, beliefs, and your impact on others and your employees recognize this through the ways you interact with them and make them feel.

Unfortunately, self-awareness eludes most people. Our understanding of ourselves and our world is usually limited because it is rare that we take time to step back from our thoughts and reflect on the reality of our situations or how we are creating that reality.

Every moment, your consciousness creates the world you inhabit.
—ECKHART TOLLE

Our thoughts, beliefs, and perceptions create the world around us. There is no objective reality. I can hear many of you objecting to this because you know what you see around you, and certain things are facts! But take a moment to consider a different viewpoint.

The science of psychology tells us that our core fundamental beliefs in life are developed early from significant childhood experiences.[139] Without a great deal of conscious work, they change very little throughout our lives.[140] Most of what we learn and experience from this point onward is colored by beliefs held in our unconscious. Every experience that you have had, belief that you have formed, and opinion you hold impacts how you experience your current reality. As no two people can have the exact experiences throughout life, everyone experiences a different reality in any given moment. Thus, there is no objective reality in the way that we typically perceive it. Instead, reality is constructed within the mind and arises out of social interactions.[141]

To develop our self-awareness, we need to set aside many of our assumptions about the way our mind works and what we have learned to look inward and begin to understand how we truly see and experience the world. By pausing and reflecting on our thoughts, we can begin to know our biases, understand that there are different ways to view a situation, and question if our automatic responses, both internal and external, are the most appropriate in each moment. This can be hard to do at first. You will likely find it challenging to pause in the moment and will need to reflect on situations after the event, but as your self-awareness develops, you will find it easier to understand your thoughts and reactions close to the moment in which they occur (for example, taking a deep breath can be surprisingly effective). Eventually, you will catch them in the moment and discover you can pause, reflect, and change your reaction for a different outcome.

> **By pausing and reflecting on our thoughts we can begin to know our biases.**

Earlier, when we saw Lindsay worry that her CEO did not think she was good enough, it began with a simple worry that she might say something wrong, and it ended with her mind's prediction of living on the streets, hungry and homeless, perpetuating the negative thought cycles we all get caught in sometimes.[142] In that moment, the childhood beliefs of not being good enough affected her present reality, and she did not speak up due to this view of the world that existed only within her mind as opposed to what was happening in the moment. If Lindsay had had greater awareness of her underlying beliefs, she could have stepped away from her automatic assumptions and questioned their validity, enabling her to make a conscious choice about how to react.

Developing Your Self-Awareness

When Socrates said, "The unexamined life is not worth living," he knew that without being free to examine and reflect on your life, growth would not be possible.[143] Indeed, self-awareness is the strongest predictor of overall success for executives.[144] It is difficult to define this skill. Many people consider themselves to be self-aware when they are not. In fact, psychologists often note that people who claim to know themselves the best are often the least self-aware!

Self-awareness is an ongoing process. It is not something gained by a one-off personality assessment that categorizes you as fitting into a box or a series of letters. It is a process of reflection that takes place over years. It is a continual assessment of where you are, how you are perceived by others, and your current strengths and weaknesses. It means striving to improve by considering where your biases lie, how past experiences are influencing your thinking and actions, and how you can overcome them so that you may view the world in a more realistic way. An understanding of the human psychology that we explored in earlier chapters will be invaluable as you work to gain insight into your own thoughts and actions.

To gain insight into the inner workings of your mind, you must be fully present. The only moment in which anything can be accomplished is the present moment. As Lindsay started to pay attention to her experiences in the moment by pausing, taking a breath, and observing, she discovered that her thoughts were almost always tied up in the past or future. Most of us spend our time dwelling in the past or guessing about the future, but true insight comes from knowing who we are in each present moment and how this is affected by our past experiences and our beliefs. If we want to be authentic leaders, then self-awareness is a prerequisite.[145]

> **Self-awareness is an ongoing process.**

Developing self-awareness can be challenging, but there are steps you can take. It begins with paying attention to your present experience.

Start to notice the thoughts you have, the physical sensations in your body that might warn you of stress, anger, or anxiety. Be mindful of situations in which you feel you could have done better. We all have them—the moments you wish you said something different or waited before you spoke out of annoyance. Sometimes it is the things you find yourself dwelling on long after the event occurred that bring the most useful insights.

Start here, and reflect on, *Why you reacted the way you did. What emotions were present? Were you reacting to another person or a specific trigger?* If you do this regularly, perhaps keeping notes in a journal, you will begin to see themes occurring, and this will give you deeper insight into your unconscious reactions. When you know what they are, you can begin to change them. Without that knowledge, there is little that you can do to alter your reactions.

As Lindsay came to understand that her underlying belief of not feeling good enough recurred throughout her life, she began to see that her reactions were to withdraw and stay quiet or to become defensive if challenged. She recognized that her reaction depended on the seniority of the person she interacted with and how much she felt their power or judgment could affect her career. She further recognized that her beliefs of not being good enough stemmed from her interactions with authority figures during childhood. Understanding the stories we tell ourselves is a powerful force for change.[146]

To look deeper, ask yourself,

What people, events, and experiences in my life had the greatest impact on me? How has that shaped me and the way I react in situations today?

How have I framed setbacks or triumphs in my life?

Have these experiences left beliefs in my mind that affect my behavior?

And then ask yourself, *Are these beliefs still relevant or helpful?*

It may sound simple to ask yourself these questions, but it is hard to do. Self-awareness begins with attention but develops through sustained practice and mindful attention to your daily experiences and reactions. Be patient. It will take time. It may be the work of a lifetime.

Lindsay's developing awareness of her underlying beliefs and where they stemmed from enabled her to recognize when they occurred. By pausing in moments when they might derail her behavior, she was able to reflect and consciously choose how to react instead of reverting to her default reactions of withdrawal or defense. Her interactions with others improved, and her self-confidence noticeably increased. She had fewer of those regrettable moments wishing she had done something differently.

The Complexity of the Unconscious Mind

When I look at a piece of quartz, I am reminded of the intricacy of our emotional lives. The smooth exterior belies the fragmented nature of what lies within. Turning the quartz reveals cracks and flaws, but rather than being imperfections, they add to the beauty and give the stone a unique identity. Movement divulges a glittering rainbow of colors as the light refracts through surfaces that are not noticeable when we just glance at the quartz as an object in passing. It is the same with our internal lives; they are so much deeper and more complex than what our exterior image reveals. There are hidden depths in all of us, unknown to the observer and often unknown to ourselves unless we take the time to look within. Being kind to ourselves and seeing our imperfections as uniqueness, as part of how we have been created over our lifetime rather than something to be crushed or denied, allows us to better understand ourselves. We can better value the depths of our experience and how it impacts others.

> **There are hidden depths in all of us.**

As we learned earlier, our unconscious mind is powerful. It works hard to protect us from feeling vulnerable or experiencing negative emotions by keeping us in our comfort zone. But on your journey to becoming a better leader, you will need to stretch yourself to grow, which means you need to go beyond your comfort zone. To do that successfully, you must understand how your unconscious blocks you and makes you behave in ways that are unhelpful to your relationships, choices, and career. Only by developing this self-awareness will you truly be able to overcome your own limitations and contribute to changing culture.

Perfectionism is a great example of how we sabotage ourselves. It is all too common in scientific communities, where we have been encouraged to achieve through academia, rigorous research standards, and scientific competition. For Lindsay, perfectionism was a way of protecting herself from the possibility of failure. Logically, she knew that perfection was unattainable, but she still strove for it constantly to avoid criticism or judgment. She desired to evade the feeling that perhaps she was not good enough, because her unconscious mind assured her that if she was not, she would lose her job—the job that kept her safe. In her mind, the loss of her job would let down her family, and she would be cast out of that group, too, undoubtedly leading to her death wandering alone in the wilderness at the mercy of lions and tigers, as we saw her predict in Chapter Four. At an intellectual level, we can see all of this as extremely unlikely, and Lindsay could too. However, beneath her rational mind and beyond her control, Lindsay's unconscious mind provoked these emotions.

Your unconscious mind limits what you can achieve by subtly undermining your intentions and holding you back.

For many of us, our unconscious mind works to stop us from submitting work that is less than perfect. It makes us procrastinate, and we avoid situations or sharing ideas that can lead to uncomfortable feelings of shame or humiliation. It makes us cautious and risk avoidant.

Here lies your greatest risk in giving up on cultural change.

Your unconscious mind limits what you can achieve by subtly undermining your intentions and holding you back. It impacts your brain through the stress response—yes, there it is again—as well as your creativity and your ability to learn, innovate, and lead well. If you are unaware of when your unconscious mind is holding you back, then it will stop you in your tracks and derail your leadership of change.

Empathy and the Art of Relationships

By entering the processes of reflection and insight to develop our self-awareness, we also come to understand that we can never truly know the experiences of others. The facets of their internal experiences must differ from our own in the way that each piece of quartz is unique. Other people do not feel the same, respond the same to a situation, or think the same thoughts we do, no matter how logical those thoughts may appear to us. It is astounding to people who instinctively understand this fact that other people do not recognize this. However, large numbers of people are in a mindset that if they see it one way, then so must everyone else.

Lindsay's peer, Pascal, the CFO at BPT, was widely recognized as successful. He was viewed by most in the organization as being a steady and thoughtful leader. Yet, in the boardroom and at his team meetings, he was continually frustrated by what he saw as poor decision-making, disagreement, and a lack of clarity in the thinking of others. Although Pascal understood intellectually that others experience the world differently, when he encountered a stressful situation where he had reached a logical or intellectual conclusion, he failed to grasp why there was doubt or dissension. This disconnect led to conflict and to ineffectual decisions, which, at Pascal's level of seniority, had a huge impact on finances, product development, and speed to market of products, as well as on the day-to-day efficiencies of operations. It just did not make sense to him. How could they see it differently when all the signs pointed one way? Wasn't it obvious?

As Pascal developed his own self-awareness and gained an understanding of how he was influenced by his emotions, past experiences, knowledge, and biases, he began to recognize how differently these factors existed within each person with whom he worked. By getting to know them individually, he came to value the diversity of thinking and experiences that each person could bring to the table. He could now interact with them more empathetically, accept different viewpoints, and have greater patience with the discussions. Ultimately, this led to stronger decisions, greater alignment on his teams, and commitment both to him as a leader and to the shared goals that they reached. What surprised him most was how these results were occurring faster. Allowing the space for discussion and diversity, which he previously saw as a frustrating waste of time, reduced conflict in the team. Their commitment to decisions meant that they did not return to the table again and again. By developing himself and understanding how others thought, Pascal became a better leader, enabled diversity of thinking, and included everyone in the process, gaining their loyalty and commitment along the way.

Be Curious and Brave

Discussing the intricacies of organizational life and relationships with clients, I have lost count of the number of times I have asked, "Well, have you told him that?" or "Have you asked her what she thinks?" Instead of guessing what others think of us, our ideas, and our actions or complaining about the impact that others have on us, all we really need to do is ask. It really is that simple.

Instead, we hold back due to our fears and insecurities around being judged or others responding poorly to our question and casting us out from their inner circle. We do not ask these simple questions because they seem too difficult. This is your unconscious mind getting in the way, screaming, "Don't do it! You do not know what will happen! It will not go well! You can't ask that!" If you look past this, however, you will find that it is not actually that hard.

By finding the courage to ask these questions, both Lindsay and Pascal discovered that people usually responded very well. They were happy to share their thoughts or feelings about a situation. It was Lindsay's and Pascal's own anxiety about other people's responses that had held them back. Lindsay found that when she shared her own feelings as she posed these questions sensitively and without blame, then people tended to hear her and reciprocate.

Bringing difficulties into the open can overcome many of the problems that arise due to the false assumptions we make when we do not ask these questions. It is rare that you truly know what is going on in someone else's mind. Frequently, you assign your own thoughts and beliefs to those people, and then you act on that faulty data. Honest discussion enables both parties to understand one another and make changes. So be brave and start asking the questions, *"What do you think about this? How did you feel about that decision?"* Share your feelings honestly if an interaction disagreed with you. Ask them, *"What do I need to know about you to improve the way we communicate or work together? What would help you to know about me? Is there something I can do to help you succeed?"* Check in to see how people are doing with genuine care, not as lip service—people feel the difference. Be curious about them and their challenges. Listen deeply and without judgment, and you will find that as people come to trust your intent, they will reciprocate. As Lindsay and Pascal discovered, if you reach this level of authenticity and honesty, your relationships will develop much faster.

Perception: How Others Perceive You

To make real change, you have to understand yourself from the inside and the outside because perceptions become reality. In the same way that you need to recognize that others view the world differently from you and you cannot know what they think, you must also understand that they cannot accurately perceive your inner world. The art of influencing and inspiring others begins with you, the leader—but more accurately, it begins with how others perceive you.

What Do You Want Your Mug to Say?

Working on cultural initiatives in a male prison environment was one of the most eye-opening experiences that I have had about the importance of a leader's lack of awareness about employee perceptions. Within their own group, the prison guards were extremely forthright about their opinions of their leaders. However, like many employees, once they were in a hierarchical, authority-driven environment, such as a meeting, they rarely conveyed those opinions.

In weekly meetings assessing the needs of the prison, one of the governors (a senior leader in the prison service) graced everyone with his presence and represented leadership. This being England, tea was always served at the meeting in a number of identical plain white mugs. The leaders who were widely disliked, however, were given a slightly different mug. On the base of the mug, visible only to the rest of the room each time they took a sip, were the words "I'm a T*@#." The guards gained a small satisfaction since they felt otherwise unable to speak up, but in those moments, they clarified their perception of that leader.

My role was to work closely with groups of guards and the governors to understand the culture and needs of the system and to support the development of leadership. As I transitioned between the two, it became apparent that the leaders who received this mug were typically unaware of the contempt with which they were held. They perceived themselves as good leaders—effective, respected, and inspiring. In their minds, they carried an important message that others willingly followed.

Interestingly, these governors were very different in their leadership styles. Some were too authoritative, and some were too nice. Universally, they were seen as ineffectual and holding little grasp of the real workings of the prison or the daily experiences of those within it. Their words carried no weight, and they were essentially ignored. The only instructions from them that guards carried out were those that either held the authority of the prison system itself or those that were followed due to fear of reprisals or other consequences. In line with these observations, research indicates that 70 percent of leaders rate themselves as inspiring and motivating, but 82 percent of employees consider their leaders uninspiring.[147] If this is the case, then there is a clear issue in self-awareness among leaders.

Leaders need to be in touch with themselves and the ways others in the organization view them. Understanding how others see you can be challenging. It can reveal aspects of yourself that you may not wish to confront, and done thoroughly, it almost certainly will. Perhaps it is time to ask yourself, *What do I want my mug to say?*

A 360 Intensive for Self-Awareness

When I work with leaders to understand how they are perceived and develop their self-awareness, I will often conduct a very intensive set of interviews with colleagues, past and present, and even with family and friends. This is an intense several-day process that delves deep and negates the way most people approach standard 360 feedback, by an insistence that they hear and attend to every detail of feedback rather than, as we all typically do, just taking in the evidence that confirms their existing beliefs about themselves and denying that which does not fit.

But there are things you can do yourself.

If your organization offers you a standard 360, be mindful of self-serving biases and ask yourself if you are just following your inclination to seek confirmatory evidence.[148] Ensure that you pay attention to every detail, especially the ones that are uncomfortable to hear. Find someone who can review it honestly with you and hold you accountable to making changes.

Seek feedback from colleagues, and be prepared to be persistent because it will take time for people to believe you really want to hear the truth—especially if you are their manager! Remember, people have difficulty speaking truth to power, so the way you receive feedback will be critical. Ask specific rather than general questions so people know what you are looking for, such as, *"What do you see me doing that supports or derails our team's success? How do you think I could handle these situations better? What do you think my strengths/weaknesses are?"* The more specific you can be, the easier people will find it to give you useful feedback.

Perception: How You Perceive Yourself

In the beginner's mind there are many possibilities,
but in the expert's mind there are few.
—SHUNRYU SUZUKI

As people climb in organizations, they tend to increasingly perceive themselves as experts. This is especially true in scientific arenas, where our training is often based on deepening our expertise and becoming acknowledged in a field.

There are two major issues with this. First, by sticking within our areas of expertise, we often limit the possibilities that can exist within our mind. We are likely to give greater weight to our knowledge rather than to the knowledge of others, and this limits our ability to innovate in a research and discovery environment. The very thing that should make us great can actually become our greatest weakness, or the weakness of our team, if we do not remain mindful and intentionally create environments where we can question our knowledge and assumptions.

The second difficulty is more internal. If you believe that you are viewed as an expert and feel it is central to your position and future career, then it becomes essential to maintain that facade. Your social nature means that you are constantly analyzing what others think of you. At all costs, you need to maintain that status, otherwise people might question why you are in charge, why you deserve the promotion, or even why you are in your current role. Your unconscious works hard to protect your self-image and self-esteem, so it is very willing to participate in this subterfuge and advise you to take actions that keep you in the expert role and feeling safe.

> **The very thing that should make us great can actually become our greatest weakness.**

How, then, can we admit our fallibility and acknowledge that we don't know the answer? If we cannot do these things, then we cannot take risks because we cannot afford to fail or let people see our vulnerability. Consequently, we limit our potential for creativity, innovation, and collaboration. These limitations could spell disaster for the desired innovative culture and R&D success.

The fact is that sometimes we don't know. By acting as though we do, we restrict our ability to learn and explore new things, and we stay caught in the trap of proving our expertise. To become great leaders, we have to crack this facade, especially if we want to succeed in an innovation environment where exploring ideas and taking risks is essential to our success and that of the organization. We need to allow ourselves to be vulnerable and to let others see that we are human as well.

So how do you perceive yourself? Ask yourself, *How do I describe myself? What is my role in my team, my family, with my boss, or in my community? What are my strengths and weaknesses, and what do I value about myself?* It's important to recognize that you may be different in different situations, and this is okay. We are not just one self; we are multiple selves in different situations. This is normal and does not diminish your authenticity. How appropriate would it be to behave with your boss the same way you do on a night out with friends from your sports team? Acknowledge these different aspects of yourself and find the core parts that are similar between situations because this is the core of how you perceive yourself and who you feel you are. Then consider this alongside what you know of how others perceive you, and question, *Is this who I want to be, or are there areas that I might like to develop?*

Vulnerability and Connection

When leaders are willing to show their authentic self or their vulnerabilities, it is incredible how often I hear from others in the organization:

"It is such a relief to see that they are people too."

"I felt like they never made mistakes. I feel like I can achieve more now."

"They are more like me than I thought."

"I always thought that leaders were above it all and that I could never be like them—that somehow they knew everything—but they are just human."

It takes a lot of courage to let people see behind the facade. Sometimes it takes even more courage to look behind it yourself, but the rewards are there if you do.

It is the habit of a lifetime to protect ourselves from feeling vulnerable. From our earliest years, we try to avoid uncomfortable feelings, such as hurt, rejection, and disappointment—feelings that might tell us that we are not good enough or unworthy. It is human to make mistakes and act in ways that we wish we did not. Rather than trying to hide them, thinking that no one will understand, just remember that everyone has these experiences. It is very likely that you are your harshest critic.

We often hear the advice, "Just be yourself." Sure, that sounds easy enough, but it can be one of the hardest things to do. It's incredibly challenging to be authentic, vulnerable, and honest with our opinions and to speak up when something is wrong. It takes courage, but organizations need this now more than ever to succeed in a world that is rapidly changing around them. As a leader, you must step up to the plate! Other people will relate to your disasters and errors. People are social in nature; they want relationships and connection. Most of all, they want to know and understand that others are like them, including leaders. Even if they do not spend one-on-one time with you, people want to look up to the top of an organization and see that a human resides there—someone just like them. They will respond to your vulnerability if you can summon the courage to share.

The Impact of Being Vulnerable

I spoke at a diversity and inclusion conference recently where Jason stood up and shared his experience. He was an employee on the lowest level in the organization. He had asked his supervisor if he could attend the conference but was told, "No. It's not for you; it is only for the executives." Instead of stopping there, he pushed through his fear and asked again and again—until he was finally given permission to attend. When he stood up to speak, he shared why this was important to him. You could see the fear on his face as he stood in a room full of senior executives and shared his personal experiences of discrimination and bias at work and the impact on his life. He broke down a little as he spoke, and he looked embarrassed.

> It is the habit of a lifetime to protect ourselves from feeling vulnerable.

Afterward, he shared with me how he felt trepidation that speaking up would compromise his career or that he would experience further discrimination. What actually happened was that many of the other attendees from all levels of the organization, including the CEO, came up to him and shared their experiences, which led to real connections—and as a result, he developed lasting relationships. The experience was a revelation to him, but also to everyone there, that having the courage to be vulnerable and share your thoughts and fears leads to genuine connections and change within an organization. More importantly, it helped others to find their courage and speak out as well.

This is why I encourage leaders to be vulnerable. Be willing to take a risk by putting yourself out there because in being authentic, you will inspire others to do the same. You will create a culture where people have permission to bring their whole selves to the workplace, and you will find that people respect and respond to you in new ways because appropriate self-disclosure leads to deeper, more intimate relationships. This is true even when you speak to those who are distant from you in the organization because employees will feel a deeper connection with you.

The work of Brené Brown focuses on this.[149] As a research professor at the University of Houston, Brené has spent her career delving into the concepts of vulnerability, shame, empathy, and courage. She views shame as "the fear of social disconnection."[150] Thinking back to our earlier exploration in Part One of factors that inhibit change, the human need for connection and belonging to a group, and the impact of stress, we can see the importance of this concept to the goal of cultural change. Brené's discoveries have indicated that encouraging vulnerability at work enables people to build resilience to the feelings of shame and be more open to discussing failures.[151] This allows for greater creativity and more engaged environments, which we know are good for innovation and business success.

Why Is It So Hard to Be Vulnerable?

Vulnerability is often seen as weakness. In Western society and corporations that typically focus on strength and success, vulnerability is not seen as a positive. Emotions are rarely encouraged in corporate or academic environments, while in scientific endeavors, they can be seen as irrelevant—or worse, as negatively impacting the meaning of data. In these environments, we learn to quash our emotions and deny their existence.

It can be hard to know how much of yourself you should bring to work. *Is there space for emotions, or should you leave some aspects of yourself at home?* Corporate environments can give us the impression that only some parts of us are acceptable at work, especially when the culture is not psychologically safe. However, our emotions provide us with the data we need to understand ourselves, build successful relationships, and make clear decisions. They will be present in our unconscious mind even if we choose consciously to ignore them because they are part of our humanity. We are not one person at home and another person at work. We carry all parts of ourselves with us wherever we go.

People respond to authenticity, and authenticity requires you to be your whole self.[152] This means being vulnerable in uncomfortable settings to show people your struggles as well as your strengths. This can feel challenging, but it enables a deeper connection with colleagues, which enables you to be a great leader who people trust and naturally desire to follow.[153]

Vulnerability does not demonstrate weakness but a strength of character. It shows that we have the courage to deal with our emotions, which are often painful or uncomfortable. If we can allow ourselves to be vulnerable enough to share our emotions with others, then we open the way for them to own their emotions and manage their own reactions. We also allow for genuine human connection and begin to create the new culture toward which we are aiming. You will know from personal experience that when people are open and honest, you respond more positively to them, but it can feel uncomfortable when we first do this ourselves. We worry that others will judge us or see us as weak or inauthentic. I have found in my work that the more senior the leader, the more of a concern this is—as if, somehow, a leader should be impervious to human emotions or fallibilities!

Being vulnerable takes a lot of courage. You must overcome the basic human fears of being cast out of the group, judged, or seen as not good enough, as well as the risk to your self-image, which your unconscious mind has worked so hard to protect. As with most things in life, being vulnerable gets easier with practice. You will prove to yourself, as Jason did, that the consequences are less dire than your unconscious mind had told you. Not only will you not wind up alone in the wilderness, but you will also become more connected to others. Acknowledging your own stress helps your team understand your over-reaction in a meeting and gives them a chance to offer you support. Being willing to be vulnerable and share about your life and challenges helps others trust you and see you as authentic. In turn, you will feel more comfortable taking these actions.

> **Vulnerability does not demonstrate weakness but a strength of character.**

Vulnerability also has practical benefits for organizations. Acknowledging a protocol error can save wasted time spent on a project. Speaking up about potential failure of a molecule in discovery leads to open and honest discussion about the chances of success, and this can have major financial implications for an organization. Vulnerability, like emotion, has a surprising number of benefits for a competence that has been dismissed and even demonized in the corporate world until recently.

Embrace your vulnerability. It makes you human, inspires others to follow you, and establishes your ability to lead successfully.

You Are Not Alone

Although these issues may impact you as a leader, they undoubtedly affect many people in your organization as well. It is part of your role to model a new way if you want to create a successful center of innovation and a culture that allows for rapid change. You must demonstrate the effect of self-awareness, exemplify the importance of connection and self-regula-tion, and encourage others to focus on the so-called softer skills that are so essential to business. These human abilities are vital for cultural change, and Gallup found that "70 percent of the variance between lousy, good, and great cultures can be found in the knowledge, skills, and talent of the team leader."[154]

As the leader, you set the tone for how seriously people take this side of the business. I am sure that you have seen organizations dismiss these skills because people look up and see that the leaders only focus on strategy and process. Even when this is not the case, it is often what people think if leaders do not share their own development stories out of reluctance to show weakness or discomfort in discussing the more personal elements of their work. However, if you want people to follow your lead and develop themselves, then you must let them know that you are doing the work as well by speaking openly about it, being vulnerable, and acknowledging your failures as well as your successes.

> **As the leader, you set the tone for how seriously people take this side of the business.**

Can I Change?

Lindsay worried that it would be hard to change. Like most people, she believed that her personality was fixed, and at age fifty-two, this was who she was. We are even more likely to think this about others. From years of studying people's minds and the neuroscience behind how we think and behave, I know that the neuroplasticity inherent in your brain means that it has an endless capacity for change. It is a constant in the brain, as it is in life.

Most of us remain unaware of our own emotional state, detached and unconscious of what happens beneath the surface. If we do not bring our various emotional states to conscious awareness, then they, rather than us, are in control. They control how we act, what we say, and even what we believe. They sabotage our best intention in the blink of an eye. This explains why we think it is so hard to make change.

We all know that change involves learning and stretching yourself beyond your comfort zone. To regain some control and better understand yourself, you need to be willing to unveil what lies in the darkness.

The question is, *Do you want to change?*

Are you prepared to put in the effort to develop yourself?

Are you prepared to accept the challenges and discomfort that come with doing that?

Most people are not. But the leaders who excel are the ones who accept these challenges by getting to know themselves and the capabilities of their brains.

Putting It Together

The curious paradox is that when I accept myself just as I am, then I can change.
—CARL ROGERS

I am continually inspired by the courage that my clients demonstrate in entering into a space of reflection to fully understand themselves and how others perceive them. It is often challenging to face the shadow sides of ourselves and to acknowledge the areas in which we are not living up to our own expectations. We set high standards for ourselves and are typically our own harshest critics. It is important to accept who we are and be kind to ourselves but also acknowledge our ability to change and develop.

When leading large-scale cultural change, leaders should be thoughtful about the relationships and environment they want to nurture within the workplace. The examples that senior leaders set can greatly impact teams and organizational environments. I see leaders succeed when they adopt the following mindsets:

- Willingness to look at and accept themselves—the good, the bad, and the ugly.

- Ability to demonstrate vulnerability.

- Acceptance that they are no longer an individual contributor but part of a larger whole.

- Mindfulness toward their everyday actions.

- Understanding of how they impact others and set the tone for the environment.

- Awareness that others think differently and perceive the world through the lens of their own thoughts and experiences.

- Thoughtfulness in their communications and relationships.

- Ability to lead by example.

I have some incredible clients who exemplify all these attributes, so I know these leaders exist.

What are you doing to become one of them?

Summary

- Developing self-awareness:

  - ▸ Enables us to better understand ourselves and others and interact more effectively.

  - ▸ Allows us to recognize our unconscious limitations and prevent self-sabotage.

  - ▸ Encourages us to be authentic and honest in our relationships, which trickles down the ranks, inspires others to follow us, and impacts business results.

- To lead effectively, you need to remain curious, understand how others perceive you and commit to modeling the behaviors and attributes that you want others to embody.

- Being vulnerable can be uncomfortable, but it brings great learning and rewards for you and those around you.

- Personal change and development can be hard. That's okay! It's hard for everyone. You are not alone.

9

Building a Leadership Team

No one can whistle a symphony. It takes a whole orchestra to play it.
—H. E. LUCCOCK

The knives were out in the meeting when an argument erupted between the VP of Research and Early Development (RED) and the VP of Global Clinical Operations. The competition between these executives was evident on a daily basis, and now it was in full view as protectionism and defensiveness as the debate raged over whose area deserved certain resources.

In the next room, a similar contest played out between the Head of Regulatory and the VP of Clinical Development, who also felt they were competing for promotion. This contest looked different, however, as it happened subtly and almost invisibly. Apparent agreement and collaboration in the room were followed by watercooler conversations that undermined decisions, relationships, and psychological safety.

An effective leadership team does not result from *what* they discuss but more from *how* they have conversations, make decisions, and tolerate risk. Their ability to do that depends on their individual self-awareness and self-regulation, the team culture, and relationships between team members. How they relate to each other and resolve conflict is critical. This comes back to understanding our individual fears, our need to belong, and the ways that our unconscious minds can undermine us in the moment. It also means acknowledging the expectations of our environment and the stress under which we are operating in any given moment.

Just because you have a team of great leaders does not mean you have a great leadership team. Competition, personality clashes, and ego are just a few of the factors that can derail your progress in business and cultural change. In this chapter, we will examine some of the challenges you can expect within your leadership team and how you can build a productive leadership team that will help cocreate your vision for change.

Individualism and Team Dynamics

Many people on a senior leadership team come from roles as individual contributors. Unless they have had positive team experiences or you have taken the time to develop a high-performing, psychologically safe leadership team, then individualism will likely continue as their default mode since they have never learned any other way of operating. Part of their job inevitably remains focused on their expertise and departments—overseeing the details, delegating responsibilities, and ensuring that processes of the department run smoothly. But now they have to learn a different role. They need to come together with their peers on a leadership team and be a part of a larger whole. Together they, and you as their leader, are responsible for the strategy and development of the wider organization and its culture. As a team, you have to think bigger and let go of any attachment to your area and personal achievements.

> **Just because you have a team of great leaders does not mean you have a great leadership team.**

As VP of RED in a global organization, David found this transition difficult. He wanted to develop as a leader but was so fixated on his own achievements and proving his expertise that he constantly competed with his peers. Every conversation about resources or progress became about whatever his department needed. He could not see the big picture but only what his area achieved because in his mind, those achievements were directly linked to his success and, therefore, his career prospects.

It is easy to understand why people think this way. You rise through an organization based on your individual achievements. They get you to the top. Therefore, it is natural to believe that more of the same efforts will take you higher. It is a feat to shift your mindset from competition to collaboration, from focus on oneself to the development and inclusion of others, and ultimately, to see the ways each department contributes to the overall success of an organization. This type of change frightens people because they do not know what they are doing. We all want to succeed and do well, but we may not know how to do it, even when we can see that change is necessary. It triggers resistance in our unconscious mind, which tells us, "Don't do it. Resist it. Stick to what you have always done because then you will be safe."

"Team" is not a descriptor for most of the leadership teams I initially meet. The biggest derailers in teams are often an individual's thoughts and beliefs that are out of place in the moment. We all have them. We are all guilty of bringing out-of-place beliefs into situations where they are no longer an appropriate response, as Lindsay did when her beliefs of not being good enough led her to remain silent or become defensive. They are lodged in our unconscious mind along with our anxiety about our self-image and social judgment, and they sneak out to sabotage our best intentions. It is only with self-awareness that we can overcome them.

How One Person Impacts the Whole

I had been working with Lindsay for about six months when I met with her CEO, Joshua. Joshua shared that he had witnessed a dramatic improvement in Lindsay's ability to self-regulate and manage her emotional state as well as her reactions to certain situations. Previously, Lindsay had been viewed by the executive team as somewhat volatile and reactive, although this was in stark contrast to the way Lindsay had seen herself. Joshua explained that in meetings, Lindsay became defensive and argumentative, and this had the potential to completely derail a meeting. One issue would take on a life of its own, causing debates that lasted well beyond the meeting itself, leaving Joshua frustrated with the lack of progress.

Joshua owned up to the fact that Lindsay's behavior was a trigger for him. Once frustrated, he waded into the argument, prolonging its life and causing greater problems for the team at large. Instead of simple resolution and agreement on an issue in the meeting, other people would be drawn in and more answers sought, requiring the team to reconvene.

> **It is vital for each member of your team to understand their individual impact.**

One day, Joshua noticed how Lindsay had altered her behavior and seemed calmer during meetings. She waited to hear everyone's view before giving a thoughtful response that drew everyone together and aligned them. He said the impact was profound. They resolved problems and issues within the meetings, with little disagreement, allowing the effective communication of decisions throughout the organization, which saved time and money.

Joshua explained his original assumption that it was a team issue. He thought they would need to work through these issues by going on retreats and doing team-building exercises, which would be both expensive and time consuming. Previous challenges of this kind had taken more than a year to address and were never fully resolved. Joshua was amazed to discover that a change in one individual's behavior could produce this magnitude of change within a team. This is why it is vital for each member of your team to understand their individual impact on both the team as a whole and the other members.

You Must Be the Change

It is tempting to blame others for misunderstandings or disagreements, but there is more than one person involved in any communication. We all need to be thoughtful and consider our contribution to a situation. As a leader, you need to encourage and support your team members in doing this. We can only make changes within ourselves; we cannot force others to change. But by modeling and highlighting the behaviors you wish team members to develop, you encourage them to follow your lead. When you have teams that blame external circumstances or have conversations about other team members outside of the room, you do not have a team that is taking individual responsibility for their actions. By focusing on "the problem is Jack," they are abdicating their responsibility for the situation and essentially saying, "I don't need to change, but someone else does." Since we cannot force Jack or others to behave differently—we can only change our own thoughts and behavior—this attitude is unproductive.

If each member can see their own impact and contribution to difficulties by developing their self-awareness, as we saw Lindsay do in the last chapter, and they are willing to change their own behavior, then team transformation can happen surprisingly fast. The change Joshua saw in Lindsay stemmed from her increasing self-awareness of the role that she played in team dynamics. She went from thinking, "If they challenge me, they think I am wrong and that I have no value" to "They are expressing their views and it is not about me." For a scientist who had deep-seated beliefs in her need to be right and demonstrate her expertise, this was transformative. She was no longer on the defensive. She realized that previous conflicts between her and Joshua had been provoked by her own behavior. This shift in mindset allowed her to listen deeply and hear the congruence in the opinions being expressed without feeling challenged. Now, by identifying the common threads in her peers' viewpoints, she could create a strong and inclusive argument that overcame the various objections. By changing this one response, Lindsay had changed the dynamic of the whole team in situations where there was a lack of consensus to something healthier and more productive. This change impacted not only the team dynamics but also her relationships with her peers and superiors. It is worth remembering that one person can greatly affect the team dynamics in a positive or negative way.[155]

As we have seen, it is essential for each team member to acknowledge and understand the impact of their behavior on the team, and leaders must encourage their employees to develop their own leadership skills and self-awareness. Much of what we consider to be a team issue often stems from the internal issues that each of us carry around. Before addressing wider team issues, it is essential to help your leaders understand at least part of the journey that you have just taken as an individual to become a trusted leader. Reflect on the last chapter to see how you might support their development and self-awareness. They need to know the part that individuals play in team dynamics and come to an understanding of how their individual beliefs and reactions impact the team as a whole. They also need to understand that they only have control over their own behavior, not other people's, and that they must be willing to change themselves if they want to become more effective leaders and team members.

The Role of a Leader in Developing Team Members

A leader is someone willing to give his strength to others so that they may have the strength to stand on their own.
—BETH REVIS

If you have taken the time to understand yourself as a leader, as we discussed in the last chapter, you will be ideally placed to support your team in understanding the roles they play. They will have seen the changes in you and recognize the difference these changes have made. By being vulnerable and sharing some of your stories about how you recognized your limitations and weaknesses and made changes to your behavior or attitudes, you will create an environment in which they can be more open to personal development. People will understand the need to know themselves and take responsibility for their own thoughts and behavior.

Change within ourselves is the only change we have control over. By transforming the ways we think and behave, we alter how we interact with others and modify the impact we have and the impressions we leave.

If you want your team of leaders to become a leadership team that can work together to create change within the organization, then it is your responsibility to help them understand the need for self-development. Show them that they are capable of change, and create an environment within the team in which they can achieve it—one where conflicts are discussed openly, feedback is the norm, vulnerability is accepted, and support is offered. The assumptions that capable people will "work it out on their own" or that "it is enough that they are good at their jobs" are dangerous. Potentially, it leaves you with a team full of Davids, each working hard toward their own goal, fighting for resources, trying to prove themselves as the best and brightest, and hoping for that next promotion. You have to ask yourself, *Does this mentality develop leaders who can take on the role of leading a team and seeing the bigger picture? Does it create a team that can support my vision for change? Or does it give me team members who each do their own thing, believing that their way is best?* If it is the latter, then your vision for the organization, as well as the culture, will be undermined as they each seek to create their own vision. Rather than working toward a shared goal that propels the organization toward success, team and organizational performance suffer with too many individuals competing for leadership.[156]

Change within ourselves is the only change we have control over.

Trusted leaders can support the personal development and self-awareness of individual team members by giving feedback to individual members and ensuring that it is honest, constructive, and designed to help them move forward. Meeting regularly and dedicating time to give feedback is essential. Don't fall into the trap so many leaders do of softening feedback or avoiding difficult conversations. This leaves the recipient unaware of their failings, believing they are doing a good job. If they are not fully aware of the issues, then they have no chance to change, and you are restricting their progress and ultimately setting them up for failure. Ask them, *"How can I help you be successful?"* and ensure you follow through with the support they need.

Encourage your team members to take time in the workday to prioritize self-development. So often we deprioritize ourselves in the face of business needs, but this is to the detriment of the organization that needs quality leaders. Highlight that it is important to take time to reflect or to engage in coaching, workshops, or mentoring. Make personal development a clear part of employees' yearly goals. I've seen one organization successfully tie personal development and well-being goals into their bonus structure. Demonstrate to your team that you engage in these activities because actions speak louder than words.

While you model behavior and encourage development in your team members and beyond, it is important to acknowledge that there will be times when people are unwilling or unable to change. You cannot force the change, and you must consider if these people are ready for the leadership roles they find themselves in. We should never consider someone toxic or irredeemable without examining the factors that contribute to their behavior, but if they are given support to change and remain unwilling to do so to the detriment of the team, then hard decisions must be made. This is the role of a leader, and toxicity cannot be allowed to go unchecked or the team, the culture, and the organization will suffer.

The Role of Environment

When team members are relaxed and comfortable with each other, they are better able to show respect, discuss issues, and reach consensus. If you place the same team under stress, unless they are individually resilient, members will revert to fight-or-flight mode, and you will see destructive behaviors reappear. The needs to prove themselves, to be seen as worthy of their place, to be right, and to win come back into play. As this happens, there will be more disagreements, and people will compete to be heard as they seek to ensure that their views are present in the conversation.

It's not surprising that consensus is very hard to reach in these scenarios. We have all been in those meetings—the ones that seem to drag on interminably, going around and around with no conclusion reached or decision made. These meetings end with, "Let's come back to this" or "We need to know more." Often, if you sit back and observe, as Lindsay learned to, you can hear that everyone is saying similar things, though they use different words, and it is merely small details blown out of proportion that prevent ultimate agreement. The consensus is there, but no one can see it because they have become ensnared by their own internal thoughts and motivations.

> A leader's role is to create a psychologically safe environment that supports teamwork and community.

If the team is psychologically safe, relaxed, present in the moment, and respectful of each other, the same conversation will enable them to recognize and build on consensus in a fraction of the time. When a team has this positive mindset, cooperates, and shares leadership in a psychologically safe environment, then collaboration, the free exchange of ideas, learning, and growth can occur. Conflict is transformed into healthy discussion. A leader's role is to create a psychologically safe environment that supports teamwork and community, reduces stress, and creates a sense of belonging that allows for diversity of thinking and vulnerability.

Creating Positive Team Dynamics

As we talked, Joerg, a project team lead for microbiome research at BPT, realized that his team was not as psychologically safe as he'd thought. The fact that they liked each other and got along well was masking their internal fears of being judged, and this was preventing real conversations about team dynamics and workflow. Joint agreements in meetings were followed by individual conversations in which he felt like a teacher everyone was telling tales to, expecting him to solve their problems. His attempts to address this democratically had left others feeling upset or criticized, and he now had anxieties about bringing issues up in the group. He felt stuck and did not know how to change the dynamic. This shows that it is not just dysfunctional teams we need to focus on. Often, teams that look high functioning can have issues simmering below the surface that impact productivity and affect their ability to innovate and take risks together. Even good teams can become better with thoughtful use of simple strategies.

Simple Strategies

Make dedicated time in meetings to reflect openly on team dynamics. Ask questions like, *"What did we do well today? What frustrated you? How are you feeling in this interaction? What is hindering our success? What did you find motivating?"* When asked in a safe environment, these types of questions allow team members to get to know and understand each other better and also to recognize the impact their actions have on others. A simple introduction to these questions can be rating the meeting on a one-to-ten scale and asking why people rated it at a certain number.

Open meetings with a simple icebreaker or check-in, ensuring that everyone has a chance to speak. People find it easier to speak up if they have already spoken in a group because they feel a connection with others, and you can also use the exercise to foster community and trust.

Create opportunities for differing views to be heard and encourage constructive disagreement and discussion. I have seen some teams allocate a "devil's advocate" whose role is to raise opposing views regardless of their own thoughts. However, sincerity in dissent is always more effective in challenging other team members to analyze and doubt their own opinions, so unearthing dissent in its true form and ensuring it is well received in a psychologically safe environment creates a team norm that ensures healthy debate and critical analysis.[157]

Acknowledge and allow time for teams to reflect on failure as a way to improve future outcomes.

Encourage team members to provide feedback to each other openly and respectfully without blame and to reflect on their interactions and the underlying reasons for their reactions both individually and as a group.

Remember that it will take time to develop the trust among the team to do this. Your first few attempts will almost certainly be awkward and uncomfortable. Persevere, and explain your reasoning to the team. Get other members involved in asking questions and leading discussions. When everyone is committed and understands the reasoning behind doing these activities, it will be easier and become more natural.

"Working on developing our leadership team has transformed my perspective on how I can interact with my colleagues. I feel that I can bring more of my personality to bear. It has enabled me to share my thoughts and opinions more honestly and with more clarity, without feeling the need to qualify everything that I say. The response has been astonishing. I feel accepted in a way that I have never experienced in a team before."

Jim, a C-suite executive at BPT, shared this comment with me a month after our leadership retreat. It sounds like a great transformation, but consider further that Jim was previously viewed as the toxic team member who created conflict and reduced team productivity. Unbeknownst to Jim, he was being considered for termination due to his perceived inability to be an effective team member. Getting to know his colleagues, understanding them, and letting them understand his strengths and fears enabled him to let go of his defensive attitude and the fears that caused him to fight for his position. It also allowed him to express his interest in people and culture, which he had previously feared might make him look weak in an organization focused on strategy and profit. Within a month, he became seen as someone who was bringing the culture to life and driving accountability in the team. His personality shone through, and he shared his knowledge in ways that the team utilized to the benefit of all.

So often, we consider toxic leaders to be irredeemable and kept on board because of their technical knowledge despite the negative influence that they have. However, this transformation demonstrated the impact that Jim's internal fears had on his relationship with the team and why it is worthwhile to develop individuals and teams to overcome these issues.

If our environment allows us to thrive rather than shrink due to stress and anxiety, then the difference can be massive. The human need to belong is a huge force in how we think and behave. As discussed, our unconscious mind considers this need essential to our very survival, so it greatly impacts the way that we show up in the workplace. For Jim, it was transformative to his experience at work as well as how others perceived and related to him.

Ensure Alignment

Your team must be capable of cocreating a vision for culture, but in order for that to happen, they need to be aligned, and that alignment needs to be real. When I first started working with BPT, I was told the leadership team was aligned on the vision, strategy, and proposed change process. However, as I spoke with each of them about what that change meant, I found they were anything but aligned. Although their words matched, the meaning of those words were different to each person. Although they truly believed that they were acting in concert with each other, they were actually pulling in different directions.

I see this more often than not, and although it is usually unintentional and unrecognized, it is devastating to the goals and success of a project. Quickly, people begin to believe that their colleagues are acting to undermine them, challenge them, or prove their own worth at the expense of the team, rather than recognizing the misalignment. We all know how fast toxic behavior can spread. Even if it is just perceived toxicity and that was not the individual's intent, people act on perceptions rather than on reality.

Ask questions to ensure understanding and shared meaning. Dig deep on what it means to each person, and recognize and resolve differences. Openness and clarity avoid future conflict and misunderstanding. With true alignment in place, more harmonious relationships are possible throughout the process, and there is a higher likelihood of success.

Instill Ownership in Your Team

Helen, the CMO, inherited the global marketing team at BPT. After three years with four different leaders, this team of six and their department of 120 employees were disillusioned with change. Helen took the time to sit with the team to find out about their experiences, and the feedback was negative. It mainly constituted complaints about the way things had been done, that strategy was lacking, and that stronger leadership was required. Helen's initial response was to remedy this by creating a clear strategic plan to take them into the future and then get the team aligned behind a common goal.

As we reflected on the issues, she realized that each successive leader had probably done the very same thing. Instead, she went into the organization to discover more about the previous leaders. She found that despite the picture painted by team members, the leaders had been highly respected and competent. They had moved to other roles where their skills were urgently needed since marketing was viewed as a low priority. It was true that they had casted strong strategic visions for the department, but a new strategy came with each departure and new arrival.

By following her initial plan, Helen would repeat this pattern and give the team the same experience. Based on experience, the team's belief that she would remain in the role was very weak. Because of this, they were likely to continue old patterns of tending to their own area and trying their best to keep it functioning despite leadership changes and feelings that they were not valued. Their reasons were valid because with no consistent long-term strategy in place, if they had done otherwise, the foundational blocks of the department would have crumbled. However, due to this, they worked in silos, often on disparate and conflicting ideas.

Helen decided to begin creating the environment of psychological safety and collaboration that she wanted to see throughout the department within her leadership team first. The intention was to create an open environment in which they could discuss and share ideas. She encouraged them to share dissenting opinions and talk about what they felt had gone wrong, how they could do better, and what strengths they could draw on. With this knowledge, Helen was able to support them in developing a strategy for the department by drawing on their expertise and daily experiences. By taking the focus off individual achievement and instead concentrating on the overall departmental goals, she enabled them to function as one unit by having collaborative goals in which they would succeed or fail together. This is a vital first step. A leadership team needs to function as one; they must put the needs of the whole team and organization above their own individual aims. They can remain protective of their own areas and supportive of their staff, but they must become willing to make concessions and sacrifices for the success of the whole.

In this scenario, Helen had enabled them to create their own strategy. Her role transformed to ensuring alignment, creating balance in both the team dynamic and the distribution of power for creation and implementation of the strategy. The team was fully committed to the strategy because they owned it and were empowered to implement it when Helen was tending to other areas of business, as she held responsibility for several functions beyond marketing. Perhaps most importantly, this ownership meant that when Helen was moved to another role six months later, they continued to function as a team with a clear strategy after a new leader came in. They could hold their vision for the culture and business and continue forward without feeling continually battered by the winds of change, clinging on for dear life. Now they were sailing toward a destination, and they could do so with or without a constant captain.

> **A leadership team needs to function as one; they must put the needs of the whole team and organization above their own individual aims.**

By creating the culture that you hope to achieve organization-wide within your team first, it becomes possible to cocreate a vision for change. When the team holds ownership and is accountable for the vision, the likelihood of success is far greater. They are committed and will model the desired cultural behaviors, as you did for them. These leaders then become instrumental in creating the aspirational culture for the organization. The ownership of cultural change must sit with your team and transfer through them to the rest of the organization. Cultural change requires everyone's participation, and everyone must be accountable for their own part in the vision. The more involved people are with the creation and development of these concepts and the vision, the greater the sense of ownership and engagement.

Outside Perceptions

Perception of your leadership team within the organization is critical. Poor relationships, bad behaviors, and a lack of alignment can leave a negative impression with colleagues and stakeholders outside the team. Research indicates that stakeholders are up to 2,000 times more likely to see teams that are perceived as having strong relationships as being effective in delivering results.[158] The culture, environment, and relationships within a leadership team are major determinants in how it is viewed from the outside. One toxic member can be all that it takes to shatter high performance and the "brand" of a team.

The ability of your team to work together and retain alignment and ownership of the change is of greater importance in a cultural change than it is in the more strategic or process changes that you implement regularly. Changing behavior is slow. We have seen the barriers to cultural change and the underlying neuropsychological processes that predispose us to resistance. Anytime the people in your organization look up and say, "Well, they are not doing it, so why should I?" it will create greater resistance. People do not like being told to do something when the people giving the orders are not capable or motivated to do it themselves. Acknowledge that cultural change will take time, and the opportunity to stray from the goal or misalign with your colleagues is greater over time, especially if relationships deteriorate.

Ineffective teamwork at senior levels has huge costs to an organization, both culturally and financially. It erodes trust in leadership and creates anxiety in the organization, causing damage that is hard to undo. At current salary rates, an hourlong meeting of ten executives is costly if discussions and decisions are needlessly drawn out. In these days where everyone is being encouraged to do more with less, these costs are rarely considered. However, the reality is about thirty less hours spent on disagreements in one team over the course of a year due to ineffective teamwork could pay for another scientist—or possibly two—at your organization or save an existing job.

One toxic member can be all that it takes to shatter high performance and the "brand" of a team.

To maintain the quality of your team dynamics, you must be able to have open and honest discussions not just about the business and scientific challenges but also about team dynamics and how you work together. Individual relationships and the conflicts and personal issues that exist must be discussed openly and frankly to ensure resolution. Without this dynamic in play, there will always be underlying currents that threaten to undermine the working practices of your team and the way they are perceived.

Developing Trust and a Psychologically Safe Team

If you want to develop a team of leaders you can trust and with whom you can cocreate a vision, then you will need to support its evolution into a "leadership team" and help members overcome the issues that individually hold them back. The relationship that you have with each member is key to this process. In my years as a psychologist and coach, I have seen how self-awareness and insight into the way we behave are essential to our personal development. I have also seen that without a strong, trusting relationship, people do not gain any insights. Instead, they put up defenses and deny the negative aspects of themselves. We hesitate to admit those things to someone we do not trust, and in many situations, we deny it even to ourselves. In other words, trusting relationships are key to change.

If you want others to trust you, then you must be seen as authentic, morally and emotionally intelligent, and in alignment with your values and beliefs.[159] Your actions should match your words, and this applies to your team as much as it applies to you. Good leaders know that supporting each person to become a leader in their own way adds value to a team because it brings diversity and freedom of thought. When we try to micromanage a process or a person's development, we damage that trust. Micromanagement can happen at any level of an organization, from the most junior supervisors to even the CEO. But remember, micromanagement creates the same feeling as being stalked by a tiger in the jungle—a lurking sense of dread and fear that produces the stress response and shuts down the cognitive capacities.

Developing your leadership ability means trusting the team around you and supporting them to succeed. It means being vulnerable enough to have honest discussions about both work and team dynamics. Your team needs to develop these skills as they transition to a leadership team mindset. It means recognizing the insecurities within themselves as well as the emotional roadblocks that cause them to revert to micromanagement or abandoning their management responsibilities when they lack certainty or direction. At senior levels, the mindset must shift out of the day-to-day and into a higher-level strategy. The role is no longer to just "do" but rather to educate and develop those around you and plan for future success of the team and the organization.

> **If you want others to trust you, then you must be seen as authentic, morally and emotionally intelligent, and in alignment with your values and beliefs.**

It takes groundwork to build a team that is capable of this. It is important to acknowledge that it will take time and feel uncomfortable at first because we are not used to openly discussing our feelings and frustrations with colleagues in corporate environments. If you are leading a team, you are likely to feel uncomfortable, even if you wholeheartedly believe in it yourself, because you will still wonder what everyone else will think.

Often, it takes the implementation of structure and rules to hold a team accountable until the behavior becomes natural. I have worked with many teams who have implemented a charter outlining the types of behavior they feel will lead to their desired outcomes. They say they will be respectful, address conflict quickly, communicate openly, and be time efficient, and too often they stop here. But it is important to know that simply stating a behavior will not make it happen. There must be structure in place for people to follow until they become used to doing things differently. There must be rules that people can be held accountable to and methods of ensuring accountability and adherence to the desired behaviors.

If you want everyone's voice to be heard, acknowledge that strong voices can dominate, that women are less likely to speak up if men speak first, and create a team strategy to overcome this. Assigning a rotating chair to ensure no one dominates and that quieter people are invited into the conversation can work well.

Simple strategies like allocating a timekeeper or having a clear agenda and sticking to it can be extremely effective as it creates shared group norms.

If you want to learn from failure, dedicate time for this, and have each member acknowledge and discuss a failure, ensuring that responses are both judgment and blame free. Moving forward, leave time in each meeting to ask if there have been failures you can learn from, and agree on a strategy to enable you to delve deep.

There is no set standard for the creation of a charter or team behavior and rules. Strategies should suit the needs of your team and its personality, so make them as unique as you are.

It takes time for people to become comfortable with new behaviors, and practicing within a structure is one way to create comfort with new habits and ways of being. A charter should be an active document, referred to regularly and given more than lip service. Reading it at the beginning of meetings is not enough; it is there to guide your actions and support your team culture. Once the team is comfortable, you can release the rigid structure, but remember to keep yourselves accountable by regularly discussing if you are adhering to your charter or if strategies need to be adapted for the new maturity of your team. It is critical for strategies to be explicit, spelled out carefully and agreed upon in advance so that everyone feels comfortable taking these measures and no one feels penalized when it happens to them.

> **Most change, innovation, and progress come as a result of human relationships.**

When Lindsay undertook these ideas with her team, she was concerned that they would think it a waste of time. What she discovered was that although it was awkward to start with, her team felt a sense of relief when she had taken this step because it helped them overcome team conflicts they knew to be issues but had not known how to resolve. It is often a surprise to leaders to discover that many people feel this is important but have never felt able to speak up about it in corporate environments.

Lindsay's conviction that focusing on people and culture was essential to the business, and her leadership positioned the team to be willing to trust the process to catapult them to a better team culture and greatly improved working practices and relationships. By bringing an element of humor to their charter by having funny ways of calling out behavior, team members were more willing to do so and less offense was taken as the tone remained lighthearted.

Building a team culture of this nature that endures beyond the individual members is essential as teams must be able to absorb new members, function as a whole, and build relationships quickly in the face of continual corporate changes. Without a psychologically safe environment and trusting relationships, the team dynamic may deteriorate over time and won't be able to successfully adapt to changes in membership or working practices.[160] Spending time on team culture accelerates trust between members, especially for virtual teams, and high trust increases project performance, team satisfaction, effectiveness, and cohesion. Most change, innovation, and progress come as a result of human relationships. Yes, hard work is important, as are knowledge and skills, but as organizations increase in size and complexity, the ability to interact with and rely on people becomes imperative. We must trust them to understand our vision and work effectively with us.

> **The era of authoritarian leadership has passed.**

As Lindsay came to understand, a CEO or leader of any large organization can no longer hold all of the threads or hope to understand every aspect of the business. We see many try and fail, reverting to micromanagement and control in the face of their own concerns or lack of knowledge of how to do it differently. As they do so, they instill fear throughout the organization, leading to the issues we have discussed throughout this book and undermining the very success they are seeking. The era of authoritarian leadership has passed. To succeed, Lindsay knew that she must rely on teams of people to support her in moving fast enough to keep up with the changing marketplace. She had to do what so many leaders struggle to do and place her trust in her people to understand and commit to her vision and enable them to trust her.

Personal Accountability and Team Responsibility

As a leader, you are responsible for creating this team and putting these ideas into action. Too often, I see teams take great steps with an external facilitator at a workshop or retreat only to return to work and resume their old dysfunctional ways. This can happen even when they are enthusiastic about their progress. Sometimes it is the pressures of organizational life, meaning other issues get prioritized. Sometimes the team simply does not know what to do themselves. External facilitation is great, but if the team does not know how to implement the ideas or their attempts to do so fail to produce the expected results, then they can become discouraged or believe it does not work.

In a scientific community where people are often accustomed to being proficient and intellectually agile, this can be particularly disheartening. It leads them to give up or conclude that it must not be for them rather than say that they do not know or ask for help. This is perhaps the failing of consultants or facilitators who do not equip the teams for long-term progress or do not provide adequate follow-up support for questions when a change inevitably fails to go according to plan. But perhaps the most common reason teams fail to drive this to success is that no one takes responsibility for it. *Whose job is it to ensure that ideas get moved forward in meetings and relationships and the work that occurs? Who holds the team or individual members accountable for the behaviors that disrupt or derail their ability to work together harmoniously?* The answer is often no one. It does not fit in the standard job description. Team members are not at every meeting, so it cannot be one person's responsibility. Instead, everyone must take responsibility, participate, and hold themselves and others accountable for the stipulated behaviors and

> **Regardless of how uncomfortable it may be, you must step up to hold people accountable.**

outcomes. Initially, until it becomes a normal behavior, this will require structure, such as inclusion in a team charter, where it is written down, agreed upon, and referred to consistently. Without this arrangement, there is little hope of progress.

You must ensure accountability for the development of behaviors that you want to see in your team. Take time to check in on how leaders are viewed by the organization at large. *Do their words match their actions?* If you want to transform culture, then those at the top of the organization must model the desired behaviors. This sets the scene for what happens throughout the organization and creates beliefs that become held by employees about what is expected and how to behave, which are the very basis of culture. *But how often do you see toxic leaders retained because of their technical expertise, intelligence, results, or experience?* The impact of toxic behavior on team functionality, business results, and culture should now be clear to you. You cannot afford to tolerate behavior that does not support your cultural vision and business goals. Regardless of how uncomfortable it may be, you must step up to hold people accountable and ensure that this accountability filters down through the organization, starting with your team.

Putting It Together

The transition to a senior leadership position is particularly challenging. It requires releasing your grip on day-to-day issues and, instead, having absolute trust that your team can work together to create strategy and keep connection with the business issues at hand. This allows your focus to move to a higher level of visualizing and strategizing for the future.

Most people never manage this, even after years in a CEO role.

It takes self-awareness and a willingness to let go of what worked in the past to discover what will work in the future. This process is uncomfortable.

As we know, discomfort leads to fear, and fear prevents us from doing many things, whether we are consciously aware of it or not.

As you think about developing your leadership team, remain aware that for many people on your team, this may be the first experience they have working at this level. The mindset shift from individual contributor to leadership team player is challenging and contrary to everything that they have learned so far, which is embedded in their mind as the only way to succeed. You are asking them to stop competing with other team members, which they see as necessary to prove that they are the best person to get the next promotion, probably to your role, of which there is only one. What serves an individual is not always best for the group. You are asking them to rise to the challenge of overcoming their internal fears and beliefs, to work in a different way, trusting that this will be best for them and the organization. To do this, you will need to draw on your own experiences of self-development to create an environment in which they are safe to learn and explore this new way of being. You must understand and support them in the challenges they will face.

If you want to create cultural change at an organizational level, then you need your leadership team to create momentum and enthusiasm around that vision. I see a lot of interest in psychological safety and building strong organizational cultures, but finding leaders who can "walk the talk" is the genuine challenge. Leadership teams are often good at casting a vision, but their follow-through can be weak. It takes time and commitment to help people envision a change, but you also need to live the message that you espouse. I know this can feel challenging in the face of day-to-day demands at work, but if leaders do not step up to the challenge and participate, then what message does that send?

Summary

- To drive cultural change, you need a cohesive leadership team and not just a team of leaders. They need to be committed to the idea of change and willing to participate fully.

- As a leader, your role is to:

  - Create the culture that you want for your organization within your team first.

  - Lead members as you want them to lead and inspire them to develop themselves.

  - Understand the challenges they face in transitioning to a leadership team mindset.

  - Cocreate a vision for culture and change and ensure that the team holds ownership and accountability toward it.

  - Help them understand external perceptions of the team and how this affects their influence.

  - Support the development of your leaders and the culture of the team by holding them accountable to "walking the talk."

10 | Setting the Scene for Engagement

The fool tells me his reason; the wise man persuades me with my own.

—ARISTOTLE

The worldwide anxiety produced by the COVID-19 virus in 2020 is an interesting example of how knowledge spreads and creates mindsets. For most people, their first exposure to information about the virus stemmed from the media, who are great fans of fear and uncertainty because it sells news. However, in the mind of the reader, it creates stress and stimulates all our self-protectionist behaviors. At an individual level, we become concerned with what it means for us.

Without the certainty of knowledge, differences of opinions are based on our individual and internal reactions to the stressors that we face. We form into broad groups that see the world in different ways: those who resist and protest, those who withdraw and disengage, and those who calmly try to understand the evidence to work logically through the possibilities.[161] However, everyone responds to their own internal beliefs around how to manage situations, fears, and uncertainties. The problem is that as differences emerge, people become more polarized and set in their opinions. If you try to overcome fear or anxiety by pushing an agenda that conflicts with what others believe they need, then resistance emerges, and they become even more set in their beliefs. Usually, this reaction results from a lack of understanding, limited knowledge, or uncertainty around how changes or proposed solutions will affect them.

The 2020 pandemic exemplifies this on a global scale. As a novel disease, there was a lack of data and uncertainty around its future progression or probable impact, and it was beyond the control of most people to bring about a solution. This is an extreme example of uncertainty in the face of change. It affected everyone everywhere, and the lack of knowledge was endemic. The differing responses by governments around the world only created greater uncertainty and anxiety as people wondered which approach was right. In fact, many came together as groups to form powerful movements against changes in response and, in doing so, increased the confusion. Underlying all of this is the individual response to change and uncertainty, and our physical stress response.

Unlike in a global pandemic, as you approach cultural change in your organization, you can prepare and even remove many of these uncertainties and triggers of stress. However, experience tells me that leaders and organizations rarely think about doing so. Usually, new ideas for change, like Ted's IT solutions, are presented to organizations as a *fait accompli*, which provokes all the same internal fears and resistances as in the pandemic, albeit on a smaller scale.

Can it be done differently? Unless you have left it too long and your organization is struggling in the marketplace or at risk of going under, then you have the opportunity to approach mindsets and inclusion ahead of time to truly think about the impact on how people will receive change.

The Usual Approach

I frequently see organizations attempt to change culture by imposing a vision from above. Typically, leaders are very thoughtful about creating their vision. Often, they engage consultancies to support them in crafting a vision and setting out a plan for change, but it is designed and introduced to the rest of the organization as a done deal to which no changes are permitted. As we learned from Ted's experience in Chapter Two, this approach provokes anxiety, creates stress, and sets up resistance. Unsurprisingly, this top-down approach is usually unsuccessful.

> **Culture is a complicated reality because there is no one method of change.**

Culture is a complicated reality because there is no one method of change. Regrettably, it is often mischaracterized as straightforward, with leaders resorting to simple adjectives to describe what they hope to achieve. We overuse words such as "productive," "agile," "inclusive," and more recently "psychological safety," but we do not define outcomes or the methods of creating this culture. We do not help people understand what it means for their day-to-day reality at work. This leaves the vision feeling disconnected and abstract, with little acknowledgment for the tension between the present and ideal culture. Rather than motivating, it can feel foreign to the reality of employees' day-to-day working lives.

The Power of People and Groups

A vision is not enough because change requires action. It requires good leadership at all levels of a company, not just from the top down, and most importantly, it requires knowledge of what each individual can do to create change and practical structures to support them. When planning your organizational change strategies, whether restructuring, merging, or changing culture, you need to think about individual neuropsychology and the power of people and groups.

Change ultimately relies on the participation of individuals, so you need to understand why employees will resist your plans and consider how to overcome this barrier to successful change. Having a vision for change is great, but cultural change takes the participation of the whole organization and everyone in it. For this to succeed, everyone needs to be on the same page, but more importantly, they need to be engaged with and committed to the ideals laid out in the vision. This is very unlikely to happen if you impose a vision from above and tell people, "This is how it's going to be."

To create an environment where individuals engage with change, you have to elicit the support of the group at large so that the most dominant view becomes the one for change in the direction for which you are advocating. Without this, you will encounter resistance. Because people are influenced by the groups with which they most closely identify, it is vital that you learn about the differing groups within your organization and the influences they have. You need to have support within each of these groups to avoid the formation of factions. As I am sure you are aware, negativity spreads more quickly than positive outlooks, so one negative person can have a tremendous impact within a group.

Left unattended, the messages of doubt and skepticism can rapidly spread. Putting thought and attention on this early and often can change the game in your favor. If you can identify the informal influencers within your organization and engage with them as thought partners, then those few people can create a social epidemic that supports the message you want to share.[162] Remember that a leader is not always related to a hierarchical status. Situational leaders are found throughout organizations. They are closer to the action, and they often have greater sway in changing ideas and behavior than a distant senior leader. These people are trusted and respected in the organization, regardless of their position in the hierarchy. Don't assume you know who they are, because research has demonstrated managerial

> **A leader is not always related to a hierarchical status.**

inability to identify influencers, and influence is rarely linked to senior-ity.[163] To find them, do your due diligence. Ask employees who they turn to for information, and seek out people who might be willing to support your communications with enthusiasm and energy. If you engage them early and treat them as cocreators of the vision alongside your leadership team, they can be a powerful force for change.

Remember that humans see new as dangerous. We don't know what it looks like or what it means for us, so we automatically assume it is better to avoid it! Throughout the world, there are examples of people maintaining the status quo rather than changing for a positive outcome because of their fear of the unknown. People stay in abusive relationships and do not leave jobs that they hate. Organizations with a history of innovation, like Kodak, become complacent in their success and stop listening to those buried in the hierarchy who see the problems coming because they do not want to change what has been a winning formula.

As we move to introduce a new idea to an organization, we must remain aware of the thoughts, reactions, and potential resistances that are at play within groups, individuals, the organization, and society at large. New ideas are not welcomed by whole populations simultaneously. Rather, they diffuse through a population as increasingly larger subsets adopt behaviors and mindsets until they become the new norm and a new culture is established.[164] Scientifically informed behavioral change and methods of communication can make a difference. The language we use, the timing of our announcements, the level of trust in the organization and leaders, the level of knowledge people hold about new concepts and ideas, and the way we use influencers all make a difference in how cultural change is adopted. By understanding and designing cultural change using the principles of neuropsychology, social systems, and individual psychology, we can avoid many of the issues that typically stand in the way of successful change.

Is "Buy-in" Too Late?

Many excellent models for change posit the need for "buy-in" at an organizational level.[165] This notion suggests that you must develop a vision for change and sell it to the organization or convince everyone that they should get on board with your idea and follow it. In principle, this makes sense because the group at large comes to accept the idea, which allows progress to be made. The difficulty is that it triggers resistance in the ways that we have previously examined. People do not like change that is imposed upon them, that feels beyond their control, or in which they have no input. It provokes their stress responses and shuts down their cognitive capacities, negating the possibility for real engagement.

As a psychologist and at a fundamental level, I see getting buy-in as a step too late. Rather than provoking resistance, we want to achieve engagement with our ideas and visions at an earlier stage of change, where resistance never raises its head. If we can do this, we can bypass the struggle to get an idea accepted. Instead, we will have employees asking how they can participate in the change because they want the change and understand its meaning and benefit to them. *How much easier would this be?*

> We want to achieve engagement with our ideas and visions at an earlier stage of change, where resistance never raises its head.

In several organizations where I have supported cultural change, it began in just one department. The engagement of employees and their enthusiasm about the topics was so contagious that soon other departments were asking, "Why are we not doing this?" or "How can we create these changes ourselves?" or "Why is that department getting to do this and not us?" The answer to the last question is almost always the drive and commitment from the individual leader or leaders of that department and how they approached change.

So before you start developing a vision to introduce and "sell" to your organization, there are earlier steps you can take.

Where to Start

The Importance of Modeling the Change

This book focuses on how you, as a leader, can be the one to lead and model cultural change in your organization. It is certainly not the only way to approach cultural change, but if you are initially the lone voice advocating for this type of change, then this method is the most practical way for you to begin. As a leader, you know that you cannot do it alone. Eventually, to create change, you require everyone to be involved.

We know that culture is primarily formed by the actions, beliefs, and attitudes of every individual. We know that people are driven to belong to groups, and those groups have leaders. Furthermore, people follow leaders and model their behavior if they trust and respect them. In this sense, it is important that your organization can trust you. In every interaction you have, the other person is constantly evaluating "Can I trust you?" and "Do you trust me?" As discussed in previous chapters, if your leadership team does not address its own development, teamwork, and ability to communicate consistently, then the rest of the organization is likely to resent and distrust the team as they cannot model the behavior they are asking of others.

Leadership sets the tone for the change, but keep in mind that you do not have to get it perfect at first. It is okay to own the fact that you are learning too, and this is a process in which you will all make mistakes along the way. Being transparent about this will give teams and junior employees the confidence to try it themselves, even if there is a risk of failure or they do not know exactly what they are doing. To be authentic and trustworthy, it is better to own your uncertainty than to pretend you have all the answers.

Understanding and Engaging Individuals

As you introduce new ideas and concepts, you want to know how they will resonate with your audience. As we know, new things induce fear or stress responses in most people and cause the resistance we wish to avoid. To prevent this, you need to understand the problems people are facing in their day-to-day work. This requires you to see the world from differing perspectives and empathize with other people's realities.

It is better to own your uncertainty than to pretend you have all the answers.

For Lindsay and most of her executives, this required a transformation in their thinking and a willingness to be vulnerable. They realized that making assumptions from the C-suite and reading literature on the subject gave limited information. Their recognition that the people who live it every day are the true experts on the organization's culture made them step back and take a different approach. Although they already knew this at an intellectual level, they had typically taken little action based on that knowledge. They decided that they needed to investigate the organization to truly understand their employees' experiences and pain, and they did so by developing surveys that hit at the heart of the issues. They also involved the whole organization in identifying these issues and developing solutions. We will look at how they did this in more depth in the next chapter. The key point is that they had to question whether the people really wanted the solutions the leaders believed to be positive. Failing to ask this question or relying on faulty assumptions leads to the results that we saw Ted experience earlier. When he happily presented his solution, his employees universally rejected it because they were excluded from the process and felt misunderstood.

Educate Your Organization

Before you can find out what people want and allow them to participate in an informed way, you must educate them. You cannot ask people for an opinion without ensuring that they first understand the issue. You only have to look at the example of Brexit to see how wrong that can go!

Cultural change is likely as new to you and your leadership team as it was to Lindsay's group. As scientists and business leaders, they were not experts on people and culture. To craft a vision and put it into action without abdicating responsibility, they had to learn a new way of thinking, and you will too. The best thing you can do is be transparent. Share your thinking and learning with the organization. Include them in the learning process, and allow them to develop their thinking alongside you. Your informal influencers throughout the organization can have a big impact here. Give them additional education, and support them to deliver it throughout the organization. The messages will spark more interest and elicit less anxiety than from senior leaders and will support your own communications.

As Ted realized with the rejection of his ideas, how can you expect people to respond to something that you present in an hour in the same way you did after spending months evaluating concepts and ideas? This is especially true of highly educated and analytical people like scientists. If Ted had been inclusive from the start, let his employees learn alongside his leadership team, and let them educate him about the practical struggles they experienced, then resistance may not have reared its ugly head so strongly. This requires a little vulnerability; it means admitting you don't have all the answers, which can be uncomfortable for many executives. However, allowing a little more time to include people and develop solutions they feel comfortable with can save a lot of time and resistance as the change goes into effect.

Neuropsychological Priming

How can you help others to learn new ideas and transform the organization without triggering internal and group resistance?

The key is to prime the organization and engage them in the conversation and development of the vision. For cultural change, this can take six months or longer, but it is well worth the investment. Neuropsychology is concerned with understanding how the brain and nervous system influence our individual thinking and behavior.[166] Throughout this book, we have considered the impact of our underlying neural mechanisms on the ways people seek to protect themselves, belong to groups, respond to stress, and resist new ideas that they perceive as challenging their status quo.

With neuropsychological priming, we are looking at ways of introducing ideas without triggering these defensive mechanisms by exposing people to the concepts that we want them to accept.[167] Over our lifetimes, we build up mental concepts and representations based on our past experiences.[168] Earlier, we discussed how our childhood beliefs are strengthened by repeated exposure and how we build connections between concepts through the physical, neural structures of our brain. The same thing happens with any information. When we are exposed to it, we try to categorize it in our minds.[169] We link the concept of cat and dog as "animals" and add them to our existing mental database of animals. When we see a novel stimulus—perhaps our first cow—we might fear, "Will it harm us?" When someone explains the stimulus to us or we recognize it as an animal, then we can categorize it, and we have greater information on which we can base our reaction. For example, a cow is an animal, it has no claws, and it runs away from us. Knowing this, we conclude that cows are unlikely to harm us, and so we become less afraid.

When we apply this knowledge to organizational change, knowing how people react to new information without enough information to reach a positive conclusion, we can then comprehend why resistance occurs and what we might do to preempt it. As part of an overarching cultural change at Lindsay's previous pharmaceutical company, the leadership team had announced their intention of converting to a "coaching culture." Everyone had heard this term, and they knew that it was supposedly desirable but knew very little about what it was or how it would impact them. The result of the announcement was skepticism and resistance.

Individuals questioned whether they had the skills, as managers, to coach others. And what would happen if they didn't? Would they be a poor fit for the new culture? Fears around job loss abounded, and people became insecure in their abilities. Because no mention of training had been made, people wondered what the future would look like. Subversive groups formed, subtly undermining the process, but no one voiced concerns due to fear that leadership would punish them for not being on board. With no discernable objections, management assumed their idea was generally accepted, and they paid little attention to the level of engagement. However, there was limited uptake when programs to introduce the coaching culture were rolled out. The seeds of resistance were already sown. Reflecting on that experience, Lindsay feared that something similar would happen as she tried to make cultural changes at BPT.

With no "tiger" in the room, people can use their higher cognitive capacities to analyze the idea.

By taking an early approach to engagement and using neuropsychological priming, we bypass many of these issues. We can use the ways in which memory and mental representations are built to expose people to new concepts and ideas. Early education on a topic with no proposed change gives people exposure to an idea without any threat to them. Their neural defenses and physical stress responses are not triggered. With no "tiger" in the room, people can use their higher cognitive capacities to analyze the idea. People do not have to make an immediate choice, and there is no pressure. They have time available to process the ideas.

It is immensely beneficial to consider the different ways individuals think and process information. For example, some people enjoy thinking and making decisions on the spot, while others need time to process things. This approach allows for both and more. People generally need repeated exposure to something before they accept it. In the sales and marketing world, the "rule of seven" suggests that consumers need to hear a message seven times before they even consider taking action.[170] By introducing your ideas slowly and repeatedly over time and in differing formats, you create acceptance and understanding. Later, when you present it as a more formal vision for the organization, people have already had time to process the ideas, and they have a mental representation of the concept. They do not fear it because it is not new to them.

Conversely, a representation that is developed under stress has a fear response as the first impression. This lays a foundation on which greater animosity will develop toward the concept over time. Our unconscious mind is good at seeking out confirmatory evidence for our beliefs and ignoring evidence to the contrary.[171] So first impressions count. This is the first step in any change but especially in cultural change, which almost entirely depends on the beliefs, attitudes, and participation of individuals. Allow people the opportunity to interact with the information, learn about new concepts, and rationally process their responses before any threat is raised. If people understand what you are talking about because they were previously exposed to the concepts, then you will encounter far more engagement with your ideas because you have not activated their defensive responses.

Putting Neuropsychological Priming into Action

Most leaders and teams who work with me go through the process of understanding how cultural change works. Lindsay's team developed an initial hypothesis and a plan that described where they would like to end up. They selected a foundational area of culture, psychological safety, which they believed was most relevant to their business. Because psychological safety underlies and enhances so many other aspects of culture, scientific endeavors, and business processes, it is the choice that I see most often from life science and biotech organizations. However, organizations also choose other areas that impact culture, such as communication, well-being, coaching, or learning to begin with. There is no right path because leaders are charged with developing an approach that is right for their organization in the present moment.

At BPT, Lindsay's team accomplished the neuropsychological priming by introducing the concept of psychological safety through a series of emails and videos. The emails shared general information on the concept, stories demonstrating vulnerability from members of the leadership team, and resources on the subject, such as simple articles, TED Talks, and research papers by scientific experts. In town halls and meetings, Lindsay's team made links between psychological safety and the practicalities of teamwork, risk, and innovation related to business success, which increased awareness that culture is intrinsic to every aspect of business and is not just a separate initiative. The leaders posited psychological safety as an area of interest to them and as something about which they were learning, and they engaged their informal influencers to shape messaging and help them understand how the information would be best received. This process of discovery captured interest throughout the organization, and employees felt if the leaders were taking the time to learn, perhaps it was worthwhile for them to learn about it too.

It is critical to do this type of education prior to running a survey or asking what people think because if they do not understand the concept about which you ask, then they cannot provide you with useful feedback. Since Lindsay's team did not merely disseminate a rigid proposal but instead expressed curiosity, they did not provoke the fears and anxieties that change so often creates.

Almost from the beginning, Lindsay's team was inclusive. In the next chapter, we will see how after educating employees, they designed an anonymous survey to elicit real experiences and opinions on psychological safety, and they demonstrated how employee feedback was incorporated as they moved forward.

By changing their own behaviors as well as organizational processes, Lindsay's team demonstrated how words and actions impact culture. Most importantly, they gave employees the opportunity to experience positive change prior to implementing a formal change process. They made it clear that this was an evolving process that could adapt as needed over time and emphasized that changes would be gradual because this was not just a one-off initiative but a long-term strategy.

People want and need to see how they play a part in change. They want to understand how management arrives at their conclusions. In being transparent about their thinking and decision-making, Lindsay's team was able to engage a large proportion of their workforce. They made it clear that culture is an effort that requires collective participation and that they wanted everyone along for the ride—sitting up front helping to navigate, not doing "their own thing" in the back of the bus.

> **People want and need to see how they play a part in change.**

For action-oriented business leaders, this approach sometimes felt like they were doing little, but taking things slowly can get you to your final destination faster. The six months Lindsay took to educate her organization demonstrated her commitment to the process and engaged her people more deeply. As a leadership team, they had hypothesized that psychological safety might benefit their organization and employees. But did they get it right? Did they truly have their finger on the pulse of the organization, or were they off target?

By taking the time to educate themselves and their organization on the concept, Lindsay's team was able to test their theory and see if others agreed with them. Now they could ask whether their employees would get on the bus and share the challenges of reaching the destination.

Summary

- Culture change needs to be addressed systemically at the individual, group, and organizational levels.

- Remember that without context or relevance to individuals' lives and work, proposed changes create fear and uncertainty and lead to resistance.

- Instead of imposing a top-down vision for culture change, engage people with your ideas as they develop.

- Neuropsychological priming allows for the introduction of new ideas and concepts without triggering uncertainty, fear, or resistance.

- By modeling the change and being inclusive, you create trust in new concepts and your leadership, and you give people an opportunity to experience positive change.

- Identifying informal influencers within the organization elicits support and demonstrates your commitment to inclusion.

- The first steps in cultural change ultimately depend on the engagement of each person, their beliefs and attitudes about the change, and their willingness to make psychological and behavioral changes within themselves to be part of a greater whole.

11 | Understanding the Current State

Sometimes people don't want to hear the truth because they don't want their illusions destroyed.

—NIETZSCHE

Einstein famously said, "If I had an hour to solve a problem and my life depended on the solution, I would spend fifty-five minutes determining the proper question." *How often do you do the same?* Most of us rush past this stage in order to solve the problem as we first see it. But spending the time to understand where we are now can mean great time savings in the long run as we avoid missteps, misunderstandings, and ineffective solutions.

If we think about mergers and acquisitions as an example of cultural work, we can clearly see that little consideration is given to the human aspects. Typically, it is seen as a numbers game, relying on reports from bankers, consultants, and internal assessments. The complexities of merging two large organizations are a given. *But how much thought is given to the views of the people within it, their past experiences and traumas, the history of the organization, and the compatibility of the cultures involved?* Paul Zonneveld and Mieke Jacobs, experts in system transformation, tell us that "good time spent early on saves a lot of repair later."[172] Identifying similarities and differences in cultures and mindsets enables a strategy for integration. We know that each of us has implicit biases and societal influences that lead us to make often inaccurate predictions about people and situations.[173] Rather than bringing preconceived notions into a merger—or any cultural change—it is vital to assess what already exists, where the strengths and weaknesses lie, and what will motivate your employees to develop an effective and innovative culture that will undoubtedly be different from what existed before.

Speak Up and Listen

One of the most common things that I hear when discussing any kind of organizational change is the issue of people speaking up. Management usually expresses a desire for people to share what they think, but when they ask for input, no one gives it. On the other hand, lower levels usually complain that speaking up is not possible because it can be detrimental to their careers and their concerns are never taken seriously or acted upon. Change resistance does not always stem from fear of the change itself but from people's anxiety that they will be ignored or have no say in decisions that affect their lives and work.

So, *how do we encourage employees to speak up honestly and share their views?*

Always Ask Questions

> *You can tell whether a man is clever by his answers.*
> *You can tell whether a man is wise by his questions.*
> **—NAGUIB MAHFOUZ**

If you want people to speak up, you must ask them to do so. Not with a generally stated desire that they should do so but specifically with questions to which they can respond. This is never more vital than when planning a cultural change. Without knowing your current state and where people desire to be led, it is unlikely that you will create any kind of sustainable transformation. Curiosity is essential to progress and innovation. Never be afraid to ask a question at the expense of appearing foolish. It might be exactly the thing that catapults you to the next stage.

Pete was new in his pharmacovigilance role, and he was keen to figure out what improvements he could make. As his first meeting with the FDA ended, he asked for feedback on how his organization was performing and meeting their expectations. The response was that they were doing fine. At the next meeting a few months later, he asked the same question and received a similar reply. He took some time to explain that he felt feedback would be useful to both parties because it would help him improve his internal processes and make the relationship between BPT and the FDA more effective. At the end of his third meeting when he started to ask for feedback, his FDA colleague said, "I knew you were going to ask me this!" and took him off to a back room to share the feedback he had compiled from various people at the FDA who interacted with BPT. He openly shared notes that described what BPT did well, where they could improve, and where they were causing frustration for the FDA. Pete walked away with a gold mine of information on how to improve processes within his organization to meet FDA expectations and speed along the approvals process. He could easily have stopped asking and taken the "it's all fine" response, as most people do, but instead he persevered. In doing so, Pete demonstrated his commitment to learning and his desire to listen and receive feedback.

> Curiosity is essential to progress and innovation. Never be afraid to ask a question at the expense of appearing foolish.

Of course, we also have to ask the right questions. Questions that are relevant to the person's life or work invite them to the conversation. They encourage participation, bring people into the process, and ignite a working relationship. This will help you understand the current state of your organization, people's real mindsets and behaviors, and the everyday work environment. It will help you to reassess your assumptions. This knowledge will put you ahead of the game. You will be able to predict where resistance might arise and how you can avoid it. If you ask very good questions, you may even get the answers to engaging people in the cultural change straight from the horse's mouth. Taking the time to do this says, "Hey, jump on the bus. Let's see if we can work out where we are going together."

If you can demonstrate that you are genuinely interested in and committed to hearing feedback from your employees and stakeholders, then they will begin to share. It may take time for them to change their deep-seated beliefs and accept that you want to know their thoughts, so persevere.

Assess the Current Reality

The majority of studies completed within organizations are quantitative, but qualitative surveys that assess organizational trends, concerns, and progress are invaluable in understanding the reality of people's experiences.[174] However, studies reported in peer-reviewed journals only have an average response rate of 37.2 percent within organizations, and qualitative response rates are typically significantly lower.[175] This may be due in part to the length of qualitative surveys. When surveys take more than five minutes to complete, we often see a decrease in response rates of 17 percent or more, and a decrease of up to 40 percent for surveys that take over 10 minutes.[176] To get quality data, we must pay attention to the design and purpose of the research.

Despite these challenges, I often suggest the development of a qualitative survey before implementing any major cultural changes. This enables leadership to assess current thinking and understand the reality of everyone the change will impact. For example, if the focus of cultural change is communication, then we can assess how transparent people feel their leaders are in making decisions, if they understand how decisions are taken, and what they feel would help them to do their jobs more effectively. If psychological safety is the focus, we can ask people for their perceptions of the current state of psychological safety, and whether people feel it is important or relevant. If we have been educating them on the subject, then people will feel empowered to comment. We will also be able to discover whether they fully understand the concepts that we have promoted and what they think needs to change in order to create a psychologically safe workplace. We can then gain input concerning their negative and positive experiences of psychological safety within the organization. For honest responses, it is important that these surveys be anonymous and seen only by external researchers who compile the data to provide themed results. It is even more important that those taking the survey know that it will be anonymous!

An initial survey we designed at BPT following neuropsychological priming and education had a 64 percent response rate. Respondents spent, on average, fifty-three minutes completing the survey, which was far greater than expected, and the amount of data was overwhelming. People rushed to share stories about how they felt, the factors that made them feel safe or unsafe within their teams, their experiences of the workplace, and what they felt management could do to create advances in the cultural topic under review.

So, *where is the difference?* I believe it is, in part, a well-designed survey. Despite organizations increasing the number of studies they conduct, many are concerned only with numbers, or they design the studies based on forty-year-old principles.[177] In fact, many organizations lack knowledge on how to create engaging questionnaires. People love to share their knowledge and experience, and well-designed questions encourage them to do that. I believe the other important factor is introducing the ideas and educating and engaging people with the concepts before asking for feedback. This is invaluable in gaining useful responses. When people believe they are being included in the design and formation of what is to come next and it is not a preconceived notion, then you will find that they have a wealth of knowledge to share.

One of the most significant aspects of doing this work is your ability to hear what is happening in the organization from the mouths of those who experience it. This insight allows you to not only tailor your plans but say, "We have heard you. This is what we understood from you, and this is the way we are responding. Let us know if we are getting it right."[178] The impact of this should never be underestimated.

Leadership Response and Involvement

There are other factors at play in this process and feedback goes beyond initial surveys to become an ongoing process in which you want your employees to trust that you care about their opinions and want them to share. To accomplish this, you must ensure that you value and reward that trust. First, you have to visibly demonstrate that you have heard them.[179] Mina, a project manager at a large agricultural organization, Agricolo, shared with me her disappointment. She had been enthusiastic that the organization truly appeared to be asking for new ideas and had emailed her senior leader, Ling, but received no response. Initially disheartened, she took the view that perhaps Ling had received so many ideas that she could not respond individually. She assumed that Ling would address her questions and ideas in a company meeting or the newsletter. Crickets! Mina's initial excitement transformed to disillusionment by this lack of response, and she decided to not engage any further. She shared that many of her colleagues felt the same.

Speaking up requires someone to be listening—it is a two-way process.

Over the years, corporate culture has tended to create strong beliefs that speaking up is not beneficial for individuals or the organization, so time must be spent to change this mindset and convince people that it is worthwhile. This belief will not change overnight.

Another question that we must all ask ourselves is, *"How often are we truly listening to what someone has to say rather than preparing to reply or waiting to confirm our views?"*

Active listening occurs in the present moment and allows us to absorb all the nuances of another person's intent.[180] Most of the time, we are in the future, thinking of a response or waiting for our turn to speak. This is just as true when reading survey responses as it is in face-to-face communication. So often we think we know what we will do, so we do not really hear the feedback unless it is confirmatory. We must remain aware of our brain's tendency toward confirmation bias and seek to overcome it. Remain open. Do not assume that you know what others think or feel. Slow down, and be present. Pay attention to what others are saying rather than relying on your own interpretations. As George Bernard Shaw accurately says, "The single biggest problem in communication is the illusion it has taken place."

> **Speaking up requires someone to be listening.**

Ask yourself, *Am I asking questions to look inclusive, or am I truly open to hearing the answers and changing my mind?*

Encourage Enthusiasm

Agricolo had invested a lot of time and effort in the initial stages of cultural change and had succeeded in inspiring and engaging their people. The lack of follow-up to people like Mina and little demonstration that they heard or made use of feedback lost them the goodwill and enthusiasm of many. It reinforced earlier beliefs that management would not sustain their efforts or follow through on their ideas. This perception is rife in large organizations, especially in these times of rapid change. Assessments are often run at huge cost, but extraordinarily little is done with the results to create meaningful change.

To combat this, leaders must be engaged in the process and committed to encouraging enthusiasm in others and demonstrating how they use feedback. This takes surprisingly little time, but because of a lack of true understanding about the impact of leaders' actions, many leaders do not recognize its importance and deprioritize it in the face of "real" business issues. Again, this comes down to your own transformation, how you behave, and how you understand the impact you have on others. Use your informal influencers and groups throughout the organization to carry the message, communicate feedback, and demonstrate engagement. This has real power. Make no mistake that employees are responsible for the real business, so do not make them feel undervalued or unheard.

> **Leaders must be engaged in the process and committed to encouraging enthusiasm in others and demonstrating how they use feedback.**

You Asked and You Listened. What Next?

Question Your Assumptions

Following the qualitative survey at BPT, the leadership team recalibrated. They adjusted their working hypothesis to include some areas that came up unexpectedly and to minimize areas that people on the ground saw as less significant. This data set the scene for everything that came next. Over the longer term, the management team's reaction to the results and transparency around its impact on organizational strategy led to a substantially higher response rate to the subsequent qualitative survey. They had succeeded in developing the belief that responses mattered by demonstrating the ability to ask, listen, and respond.

Be Transparent

The most common mistake I see, at this stage of the process, is a lack of transparency. If you do not share what you've heard, then you lose the benefit of using it because employees still will not feel heard. In fact, you will create more resistance as everyone wonders, "What happened to the results of that survey? Was it just another pointless exercise that will lead to no action?"

If you take action, make sure that people know. If it takes time to decide on a course of action, let them know that. Thank them for their participation, and give people expectations rather than being silent for weeks. Do not hoard the results of the survey, but instead, get the information out where everyone can see it. If you want people to feel included in the process, then include them. Feedback loops are essential and provide an opportunity for people to stay involved with the process. Often, organizations miss this transparency because they focus on getting results, making the next plans, and getting straight to work. But if you do that, the organization at large misses understanding a vital part of the process—the part that most deeply concerns the employees and makes them feel valued and connected to the vision. If you make a decision at the management level because it seems quick and easy, then you run the risk of resistance, and your decision will take longer to come to fruition, if it ever does. Taking a little more time to share feedback,

> **Feedback loops are essential and provide an opportunity for people to stay involved.**

invite further comment through multiple avenues, and include people will almost always result in faster change in culture.

Commit to Communication

As a leader, you need to understand the length of time it takes to make cultural change sustainable and a part of the daily experience. From a high vantage point, it is easy to feel that you have done your part and to start thinking about the next step. However, ideas and tools take time to distill and become accepted by an organization. Realistically, a true change in culture takes several years, and first steps to changing climate can take months. If you start talking about next steps before this happens, it creates uncertainty. What leaders see as responding to changing times often leaves the rest of the organization feeling that leadership has moved on to the next shiny new thing before the previous one had a chance to succeed. This leaves employees change fatigued, and no matter how good the idea, they are likely to meet it with resistance and low enthusiasm.

As Agricolo began their cultural change, they also chose psychological safety as a foundational concept. The employees came together with a great deal of enthusiasm, sharing ideas to explore ways of working and developing themselves. It went so well that after twelve months, the leaders decided to bring forward their next initiative, which was to focus on the ways that communication occurred throughout the organization. They had chosen this based on feedback from teams that a lack of clarity in corporate communications was holding back products from market and causing miscommunication and delays cross-functionally.

The leadership team clearly saw how they could build the communication strategy on the concepts of psychological safety and how this would move them forward faster than just putting in place standardized processes. However, when they introduced the concept, they failed to mention these details. Instead, they focused on what a difference improving communication would make and what they planned to do about it. They failed to reference all the work done by teams that were the stepping-stones to this strategy or how it was all part of the broader cultural change. The message that the organization received was, "On to the next thing, and back to being told how to implement processes and procedures." This left the employees believing that their time and enthusiasm for creating psychological safety in teams was a wasted effort, ignored by management, which made them feel unrecognized and undervalued.

Certainly, this does not mean that you should refrain from thinking about next steps. Simply keep in mind that when you introduce a concept, it is well worn to you but brand new to your audience. You cannot expect them to be where you are in your thinking. They need time to go on that journey, and it is part of your role to help them digest it faster than you did. By using the principles of neuropsychological priming and removing the obstacles from their path, you can help them react positively rather than with fear and resistance. It is likely that you have a well-formed strategy in mind, and your next step is a logical progression from the last. *Are you communicating this to your organization? Are you helping them see the development of strategy, or are you presenting what they may perceive as disconnected ideas?* It is vital to build those links and explain them to the organization so that they can feel connected to the strategy and understand how they can contribute. A new idea should be firmly connected to the ones that came before it. This demonstrates that you have a clear direction and creates confidence in your leadership.

At Agricola, it would have been simple and time effective to explicitly build these connections into strategy, be transparent in communication, and bring employees on the journey. Instead of resistance, Agricola could have maintained the enthusiasm and elicited participation. In times of change, leaders need to be conscious of the impact they have. Transparency in communication and visibility of leadership are crucial, as is the change story that you tell and the feedback loops you create. If you put thought into this process and take the time to truly listen to your employees, then change will occur faster than you had imagined.

If I can listen to what he can tell me, if I can understand how it seems to him, if I can see its personal meaning for him, if I can sense the emotional flavor which it has for him, then I will be releasing potent forces of change in him.

—CARL ROGERS

Summary

- To make change or solve a problem, you need to understand the realities of your employees' daily work lives and thinking.

- A process of eliciting honest feedback will give you a wealth of knowledge if you ask the right questions.

- If you want people to speak up, then you must prove that you can listen and create effective feedback loops.

- Demonstrate that you heard people, and be transparent in your learnings, feedback, and willingness to adjust course based on their responses.

- Cultural change takes time, and communication is vital. Moving on too quickly without explanation of how the ideas are connected will create change fatigue and reinforce negative perceptions of the organization and leadership.

12

A Scientific Experiment

Ever tried. Ever failed. No matter. Try again. Fail again. Fail better.
—SAMUEL BECKETT

We know that the speed of change in organizations and the world continues to increase. To be effective and survive, organizations have to adapt.[181] To be innovative, we need to alter our path and course correct swiftly and effectively. This is true for processes, strategies, and scientific discoveries, and it is the same for managing people and culture. While our long-term goal remains steady—to create environments that enable people to work optimally, share ideas, be resilient, make new discoveries, and improve on old ideas—we also need to acknowledge that we will make mistakes along the way and allow for the probability of changing direction. As with any scientific process, we need to hypothesize, test, assess, reformulate our hypothesis, and iterate.

Scientists Understand Innovation

When I look at the work that is done in research and innovation environments, I see this approach exemplified in the scientific processes at play. Over and over, new ideas are put forward and explored, and then they are either set aside, learned from, or built on in new ways as we recognize that the original hypothesis had faults. For pharmaceutical, agricultural, or other life science organizations, there are many risks on the journey from ideation to commercialization. Rates of failure are high, and so a willingness to try, take risks, fail, and begin again while learning from your experience is vital. Yet, in these same organizations that are filled with discovery and development scientists, people processes are looked at once, and there is no reexamination of whether they work. If they fail, they typically place the blame elsewhere: on an external consultant, HR processes, or a specific manager who is seen as failing. This work is rarely seen as the responsibility of the scientists, leaders, or employees within the organization. However, throughout this book we have seen that culture—and especially the development of agile, resilient workplaces and employees—takes the involvement of everyone, particularly the leaders who have to demonstrate their commitment to the process. If we accept this knowledge, then we can no longer conveniently place blame elsewhere. We must all take responsibility for what is happening.

Collaborating to Create Culture

By applying the scientific principles of research and discovery to people and culture, you can put robust measures in place that will allow the process of building culture itself to become resilient. This will enable you to learn from mistakes and failures as much as you do from successes. It provides the ability to evolve as you move forward and adapt to changing circumstances. *Can you guarantee that the plan you put in place for your culture today will be the same one that you need in five years?* No. The world changes too fast for that. However, if you have developed a plan for strong foundations within your culture, such as psychological safety, resilience, flexibility, and agility, then you will have the ability to track your progress and see how to course correct along the way.

As Henry Ford wisely acknowledged, "Failure is simply the opportunity to begin again, this time more intelligently." Yet, when it comes to people and culture, I rarely see this attitude. It is usually approached as a one-off initiative to be revisited in five years when organizations recognize that it failed to make the expected changes.

My recent experiences in the corporate life sciences show that the value of culture and people's contributions are increasingly coming to light, and many companies are now placing their focus here. The difficulty is that few people within the organizations understand the concepts behind cultural change in order to effectively produce them. Tell a microbiologist who just became a senior director to lead a team to successfully develop a novel vector platform, and they will willingly rise to the challenge because they have their own understanding and background in the area. They will see the process through its ups and downs.

> **The value of culture and the contribution of people are increasingly coming to light.**

Now ask that same leader to take charge of a cultural change, and they might accept the challenge, but as a microbiologist, they will lack the expertise to negotiate the ups and downs or recognize potential issues. This is no failing on the part of this leader. If we asked a psychologist or expert in human behavior to lead a team in developing a novel vector platform, they would be similarly unprepared. In fact, we probably would not ask it of them and would instead turn to someone with knowledge of microbiology. We have an unrealistic expectation that people who advance within an organization based on their technical skills will magically have an ability to manage other people when we give them little training or knowledge to do so. The limited learning that occurs in emerging leadership programs, though helpful, is certainly not enough to understand the complexities of human behavior and change.

We need to bring this learning into organizations. Having experts come in to run or design it is simply not enough. This knowledge must be systemic and embedded within the organization. It must become natural for leaders and employees at all levels throughout the organization to increase their awareness of these concepts. Then, as they rise through the ranks, they will not be left in the position of today's leaders, who are expected to lead cultural and systemic change without the knowledge to do so.

> **We have an unrealistic expectation that people who advance within an organization based on their technical skills will magically have an ability to manage other people.**

Everyone in the organization needs to understand the part they play, the ways they and others think and act and why, and the impact they have on an organizational system. The most successful way to instill this knowledge is through trial and error, honest and open conversation, and seeing it modeled from above, below, and laterally. We all learn better if we are allowed to make sense of information ourselves rather than having to rely on someone else telling us how to do something. We can all learn what it means to be human and lead from each other, but only if we are vulnerable enough to allow ourselves to bring our humanity to the workplace and take risks. To do that, we need a culture that ensures we feel safe to do so.

Individual Development

As we work to develop our organizations and create cultures that will enable us to succeed, we need to support leadership development for everyone. This does not mean that everyone is aiming for senior leadership. It is not just emerging leaders or top talent who need our focus. To be successful in changing and maintaining a positive culture, everyone must become a leader in their own right, no matter where they sit in the organization. For some, this may mean the traditional path of promotions and leadership training, but for everyone on a more immediate level, it means being a leader within themselves. Even individual contributors need to develop their capacities for change, improvement, engagement, and building relationships with others. These capabilities are relevant at every level of the organization, from the most junior person to the support functions and the executives. Not everyone wants to be promoted, but as humans, we all want to contribute, to feel that we add value and are accepted. We can all lead in the spaces where we exist on a daily basis as long as the culture encourages us to do so and honors our well-being.

As Lindsay's team came to trust that those below them were becoming more confident and competent, they were able to put greater focus on the higher-level functioning of the organization and perform the true roles required of a senior leadership team.

As humans, we all want to contribute and to feel that we add value and are accepted.

Executives who feel confident in the functioning of the organization are freer to manage their own lives and find a healthy balance. This freedom enables them to be better leaders because good leadership requires us to be our optimum selves to inspire others and drive change. The development of leaders must focus on who leaders are rather than just what they do. Organizations need to replace outdated leadership training programs that are typically attended and forgotten, with long-term coaching, mentoring, and development for both individuals and teams. Greater self-knowledge and growth lead inexorably to greater confidence, increased adaptability, and innovation, all of which are required to lead organizations into the future in a sustainable way.

The Willingness to Experiment

With this trust in the organization and the people comes flexibility and the ability for experimentation. Trust empowers people to take risks and try something new. Although this is important in scientific R&D, it is even more important in changing cultures. We previously discussed the importance of gaining everyone's involvement and participation. The leaders of cultural change need to be embedded at every level, and you will find surprising expertise in these skills throughout your organization since this is not typically what the average business gives promotions for. Use this expertise to identify and gain the support of the influencers within your company. People will follow people they trust and people they believe care, no matter their seniority, especially when they are supported by hierarchical leaders.[182] Interest and passion can be more important here than technical skills. Often, organizations do not have enough resources to dedicate full-time roles to people projects, so employees take on these initiatives in addition to their regular roles. As you see the value in what they can do and identify people with real skills and enthusiasm, you can dedicate the time and resources they need and reward their efforts.

The process of cultural change is an exploration and an adventure. Have enough confidence and trust in others to let them share ideas with you. If they can explain why it fits the vision, then be brave enough to let them try. Some ideas will work, some will not take off, and others will outright fail. If your leadership team can be vulnerable enough to hold up their hands and say, "We tried this. It didn't work. Let's reevaluate," then you are learning valuable lessons along the way and are demonstrating your willingness to experiment and the cultural attributes you wish to cultivate.

The Need for Transparency

Again, transparency about failure and progress is key. If you try to hide it, people will know. Employees respect honesty, involvement, and the ability to contribute to something they believe is valuable to themselves and others. Forget this at your peril! Relationships, psychological safety, and resilience are all impacted by how we communicate and our willingness to be transparent. Sadly, we rarely pay attention to this in any depth. To be honest, open, and effective in your communications, you need to be both self-aware and aware of how your words and actions impact others around you.

"Like it or not, innovation is a team sport," Amy Edmonson tells us.[183] It is true that innovation typically occurs in groups. It often requires working across disciplines and overcoming boundaries of distance, knowledge, assumptions, and status. For cultural change specifically, you cannot work in silos. To make change happen, you must include everyone and work together to develop common goals and languages. To be successful, it is critical to have honest communication, curiosity, and a psychologically safe environment where people feel heard and safe in sharing their views. These are worthy goals for any organization.

> Transparency about failure and progress is key. If you try to hide it, people will know.

A Scientific Journey

Being honest about uncertainty can be difficult because it is something that we are all afraid of at some level.[184] Bringing it out in the open to allow discussion can dramatically change how people feel about uncertainty and the trust they place in leaders and facts.[185] This takes us full circle, back to the importance of developing and understanding yourself so that you can bear the vulnerability and discomfort that engaging in these kinds of discussions inevitably brings up. Since you are now part of your own science experiment, you must watch yourself, your successes, and your failures as closely as you might observe any new research project.

In the midst of indecision or doubt, it is important to remind ourselves that many of the paths available to us can lead to positive results. There is often no "right" decision. Typically, it is our thoughts and attitudes that lead us to define a choice as positive or negative, rather than the reality of the situation. Explore what is out there, and take a chance. Each path that you choose has its own unique journey with many turns ahead, but indecision often results in a lack of forward movement.

When we analyze companies that continually excel, such as Apple, Toyota, and IKEA, to name a few, they respond to a changing environment, but more importantly, they coherently make changes that are consistent, measured, and aligned with their vision. They acknowledge culture as an important puzzle piece and are willing to experiment. If we want people to tolerate failure, then we must be comfortable with it ourselves. People must feel confident that failure is acceptable and that they will not be judged or unfairly blamed. They should feel secure in support from management no matter the outcome and know that failure will be regarded as a part of learning. We know that successful scientific discovery and innovation is enhanced by an atmosphere of psychological safety. If we create this in our organization, then we will fast track our success, but we can also use the journey to develop culture as a way to practice these new skills and ideals.

Give people the ability to take the reins of change.

Give people the ability to take the reins of change, especially those who are enthusiastic rather than just those who are in hierarchical positions of power. As we have said, leadership for cultural change and the development of individuals can, and should, come from all levels. It must have the support of management, and it must be somewhat consistent, but if you are willing to let people try new ideas and potentially fail so as an organization you can learn and develop from these initiatives, then you will be modeling the very environment you are aiming for, even as you journey toward it. You will undoubtedly find skillsets, expertise, knowledge, and new leaders in some unexpected places as you travel this path.

Ed Catmull of Pixar says that mistakes are "the inevitable consequence of doing something new...without them we would have no originality." You do not want to develop the same products as your competitors. You want to stand out in the marketplace. Why would you want your culture to be the same as everyone else's? You want to stand out here too. A unique culture will make you more innovative, it will take you to new frontiers, and it will attract and retain talent. These days, people are increasingly searching for jobs at organizations with positive cultures and values that align with their own, and a workplace environment where they can feel valued, respected, and included.[186]

By taking a journey toward cultural change that allows for healthy exploration and inclusion and prioritizes the needs of humans, you exemplify and learn the attributes of flexibility and experimentation that you want to develop for an innovation culture. If we can fail and learn from failure, if we can develop cultures where people are enabled to be flexible, adaptable, and healthy and can bring their best to work, then we will be able to push ourselves and our organizations to new heights.

Summary

- Cultural change is a scientific process requiring innovation, and this knowledge can guide us in our approach to designing and implementing change.

- We need to distill knowledge of culture and human behavior throughout every level of organizations and collaborate to develop strong foundations for cultures that support our goals.

- A focus on developing individuals and acknowledging that everyone contributes to culture will help us succeed in cultural change, innovation, and business success.

- As we trust others to play their part, we become more flexible, resilient, and open to experimentation.

- Take risks, and be willing to fail, admit, and learn from your mistakes.

- To transform culture, your organization needs to go on a learning journey. Few industries are more capable of rising to this challenge than the scientific community, if they are open to expanding their knowledge, applying their skills, and engaging in the human side of organizational life.

13

Conclusion

If, as an innovation leader, you are serious about tackling culture and recognize the role it plays in business success, then you must start with yourself.

The first thing to acknowledge is that not everyone will have your mindset. Despite growing recognition that people and culture are important to scientific innovation and organizational success, these views are not yet mainstream. Most people take a very halfhearted approach or only pay lip service, saying the right things while taking little action, if they acknowledge it at all. This means that you can find yourself as a lone voice advocating for cultural change in the face of more "practical" financial or business goals that others are pushing forward.

Advocating for change alone can be very uncomfortable. It positions you as an outsider. It means that others may judge you, and you are potentially taking a risk that will reflect on you and the way you are perceived. You will need to have faith that it is worthwhile. But more than that, you will need to have faith in yourself and your strength to see through a process that is, by its very nature, not a quick fix but a long-term strategy and solution. To be successful, you must see cultural change through to the end and not give up in the face of challenges. Have confidence that investing in people and culture will ultimately help you and your organization navigate strategic and financial challenges in the coming years. It takes courage to walk this path, especially if faced with other people's doubts, but the benefits are worthwhile.

Throughout this book I have emphasized the importance of starting with yourself. This is the foundation you will need to stay the course and hold on to the courage of your convictions to inspire confidence in those who will follow you. You will need to be self-aware and understand how your unconscious mind will attempt to undermine you in this process. We all have doubts, which are entirely natural. If you know your weaknesses, then you can anticipate them and strategize ways to overcome them to stay on your path. The confidence you have in yourself and your vision will help you build a strong leadership team who can carry these concepts and ideas forward, even in your absence. Here, you are laying the groundwork for the future success of your organization.

> **It takes courage to walk this path, especially if faced with other people's doubts.**

As cultural messages spread and people adopt them throughout your organization, you will find that many people at all levels start to advocate for what you are trying to achieve. It is important to recognize and acknowledge these people, as they are the ones who will enable your ideas to become reality. Your vision and strategy will flex and adapt as more people get involved and contribute ideas. For a scientist and a leader, this is the very essence of learning and growth. Tackling cultural change will certainly challenge you to do that!

All parts of this journey in transforming yourself as a leader and your organization share a commonality of prioritizing human emotion and well-being and the willingness to take risks and do something different. By approaching organizational and cultural development in ways that benefit business, scientific discovery, and employee well-being, we can foster environments that support people's physical and mental health.

These improvements bring further savings and benefits to organizations through reducing healthcare costs, lowering rates of absence and turnover, and increasing capacity for innovation, to name but a few. Supporting the individual learning journey at all levels of the organization, and particularly encouraging the development of self-awareness and relational skills, develops resilience, supports health and well-being, cultivates future leaders, and transforms culture.

Corporate culture grows through the involvement of every individual within it. Your role as a leader is to ensure a positive evolution that maintains the concepts in your initial vision rather than allowing it to diverge and take on its own route to another destination. Within life sciences and R&D, one goal is almost always to create an atmosphere within which innovation can thrive. In this type of environment, scientists and colleagues can share ideas, be flexible and diverse in their thinking, and adapt to meet the changing circumstances in the world around them. The culture that you create, sustain, and evolve over time will determine your success. It also means you, as a scientist, already have many of the skillsets needed to achieve it.

> **The culture that you create, sustain, and evolve over time will determine your success.**

Each organization will achieve cultural change in their own unique way; there is no set path for you to follow. As a leader, you must be willing to take on this challenge and be open to whatever comes, knowing that you have the strength to withstand the inevitable ups and downs that come with any scientific experiment.

Transformation is a journey of discovery. It involves looking at our internal attributes and overcoming the fears, doubts, and external circumstances surrounding them. It is like excavating a diamond from the rough, revealing its assets, polish, and brilliance and allowing it to illuminate the world. It is the same with people and cultures. Real growth and real leadership develop from a transformative journey where people are enabled to explore their potential and express who they are with confidence, free from the shackles of self-doubt and the constraints of expectations.

This is where innovation lives. This is where success resides.

As we enter this journey to become better leaders, stronger team players, and more innovative and successful scientists and business executives, our power comes from knowing ourselves as well as our abilities. It requires being true to ourselves, loving what we do and wanting to inspire the same transformations in others.

To find out more about the concepts in this book, I invite you to visit www.drkateprice.com. If you are ready to Tame the Culture Tiger at your organization, schedule a consultation with me to explore the key questions posed in this book and to start your journey. I would love to hear from you.

Acknowledgments

Writing a book like this is the culmination of a lifetime of experiences and learning, from childhood onward. Everyone I have encountered along the way has played a part in shaping my understanding of the world, how humans function, and how organizations and communities evolve. As such, I am grateful to so many people but especially to those who contributed to this book and the work that led me to it.

To all my clients who inspire me with their work and dedication to learning about themselves and transforming the systems around them through their perseverance and constancy.

To Aaron Schacht for his confidence in my work and willingness to read and comment on my initial drafts and ultimately contribute a wonderful foreword. To Amy Edmonson for taking the time to work with me to ensure accuracy in my representation of her ideas and research data, which are so essential to healthy cultures. To Julie Lawless, whose corporate communication skills got me over a couple of hurdles in writing the cover copy. And to those who were willing to endorse both me and my work: Nick Gray, Edward McGruder, Seth Godin, JeVon McCormick, Marc de Beer, and others. I appreciate your belief in me.

To all the team at Scribe who made this book come into being and especially my amazing editor, Aleks Mendel, whose comments helped me refine my language and convey my ideas; Hal Clifford, who helped me establish my vision from the beginning, and Liz Driesbach, for her unending patience with the cover design process.

To the clinical psychology doctoral staff at the University of Plymouth and all my clinical supervisors and colleagues over the years, without whom I would not have the breadth of knowledge that enables me to do this work. With a special mention for Rudi Dallos and Sabrina Halliday for bringing to life their systemic perspectives, which have been so key to my understanding of how individuals function both within themselves and the systems around them.

To the members of the culture and psychological safety teams I partner with who work so diligently to bring these ideas to life in their organizations in their own unique styles, and to all the scientists who let me run my ideas by them, especially Kristen Westdorp, Erika Slinker, and Kevin White, who were willing to let me bounce my organizational and pharmaceutical examples around and correct my science where needed.

To my husband, Jason, and my family for their unconditional support in everything I have done over the years, and to all the friends who have expressed interest in my work and encouraged me to write this book. And to Alex Johnson and Malcolm Adie for their dedicated support in the times I lost my way but also in keeping me sane with weekly games of Catan despite being on a different continent. To Stephen Russell and Kay Boyce-Lees for everything you did and do. And to my cats who tried to help by sitting on the computer or anything else I was trying to work on—all the time.

To my scribe fam: Kelly Woods, Ted Harrington, Ron Thurston, Lindsay Shoop, Joette Orman, Colleen Healy, Glen Robson, Sabreet Kang-Rajeev, Craig Perkins, and Hussein Al-Baiaty. Your support and the shared experiences along this journey have been incredible. I'm so happy to have gotten to know you all.

To the huge variety of people I have met throughout my life and career, you have all contributed to the way I see the world now and my desire to make it a better place for us all to live in. Thank you.

References

Chapter 1:
What Is Culture, and Why Should You Care?

1 Pir, S. (2020, May 26). Why Your Company Culture Is A Lie And What You Can Do About It. Retrieved from https://www.forbes.com/sites/sesilpir/2020/05/26/why-your-company-culture-is-a-lie-and-what-you-can-do-about-it/

2 Weaver, G. R. (1986). The "iceberg analogy" of culture. In R. M. Paige (Ed.), *Cross-cultural orientation. new conceptualizations and applications*, pp. 135–137. Lanham, MD: Council on International Educational Exchange, University Press of America.

3 Benedict, R. (1934). *Patterns of culture* (p. 46). London: Routledge.

4 Feist, J., & Feist, G. J. (2009). *Theories of personality*. New York: McGraw-Hill Education.

5 Darino, L., Hancock, B., & Lazaroff-Puck, K. (2019, December 19). Employee motivation in the age of automation and agility. Retrieved from https://www.mckinsey.com/business-functions/organization/our-insights/the-organization-blog/employee-motivation-in-the-age-of-automation-and-agility

6 Kotter, J. P., & Heskett, J. (2011). *Corporate culture and performance*. New York, NY: Simon & Schuster.

7 McCann, D. (2015, June 4). Treat Employees Well, See Stock Price Soar. Retrieved from https://www.cfo.com/people/2014/04/treat-employees-well-see-stock-price-soar/

8 Harter, J., & Mann, A. (n.d.). *The right culture: Not just about employee satisfaction.* Gallup Business Journal. Retrieved August 26, 2022, from https://www.gallup.com/workplace/231602/right-culture-not-employee-satisfaction.aspx

9 Kunsman, T. (2022, June 14). *29 employer branding statistics your company must know.* Everyonesocial. https://everyonesocial.com/blog/employer-branding-statistics/

10 Conger, K. (2019, December 30). Uber settles federal investigation into workplace culture. *The New York Times*. https://www.nytimes.com/2019/12/18/technology/uber-settles-eeoc-investigation-workplace-culture.html

11 Snyder Bulik, B. (2021, February 19). *Pharma's reputation rehab: A whopping two-thirds of Americans now offer a thumbs-up, Harris Poll finds*. Fierce Pharma. https://www.fiercepharma.com/marketing/pharma-reputation-hits-high-americans-two-thirds-now-give-positive-rating-harris-poll

12 Indeed. (n.d.). *Working at Zappos family of companies.* Retrieved October 12, 2020, from https://www.indeed.com/cmp/Zappos-Family-of-Companies/reviews

13 Kunsman, T. (2022, June 14). *29 employer branding statistics your company must know.* Everyonesocial. https://everyonesocial.com/blog/employer-branding-statistics/

14 Society for Human Resource Management. (2019). *The high cost of a toxic workplace culture: How culture impacts the workforce—and the bottom line.* https://pmq.shrm.org/wp-content/uploads/2020/07/SHRM-Culture-Report_2019-1.pdf

15 Mahan, T. F., Nelms, D., Bearden, C. R., & Pearce, B. (2019). *2019 Retention report: Trends, reasons and a call to action.* Work Institute. https://info.workinstitute.com/hubfs/2019%20Retention%20Report/Work%20Institute%202019%20Retention%20Report%20final-1.pdf; Derler, A., Cook, I., Smessaert, A., Winlaw, M., Kim, C., & Steininger, M. (2021). *Stop the exit: A data-driven approach to retaining top talent.* Visier. https://www.visier.com/wp-content/uploads/2021/10/Rep-ResignationWave-100121.pdf

16 Mahan, T. F., Nelms, D., Bearden, C. R., & Pearce, B. (2019). 2019 *Retention report: Trends, reasons and a call to action.* Work Institute. https://info.workinstitute.com/hubfs/2019%20Retention%20Report/Work%20Institute%202019%20Retention%20Report%20final-1.pdf

17 McFeely, S., & Wigert, B. (2019, March 13). This fixable problem costs U.S. businesses $1 trillion. Gallup Workplace. https://www.gallup.com/workplace/247391/fixable-problem-costs-businesses-trillion.aspx

18 Society for Human Resource Management. (2016). *Employee job satisfaction and engagement: Revitalizing a changing workforce.* https://www.shrm.org/hr-today/trends-and-forecasting/research-and-surveys/pages/job-satisfaction-and-engagement-report-revitalizing-changing-workforce.aspx

19 Kruse, K. (2012, June 22). What is employee engagement? *Forbes.* https://www.forbes.com/sites/kevinkruse/2012/06/22/employee-engagement-what-and-why/?sh=34a9183d7f37

20 Crabtree, S. (2013, October 8). *Worldwide, 13% of employees are engaged at work.* Gallup World. https://news.gallup.com/poll/165269/worldwide-employees-engaged-work.aspx

21 Spencer, J. (2020). *Data Shows Employee Turnover Is Bigger Challenge Than Hiring.* Retrieved from https://www.zenefits.com/workest/employee-turnover-infographic/

22 Crabtree, S. (2013, October 8). *Worldwide, 13% of employees are engaged at work.* Gallup World. https://news.gallup.com/poll/165269/worldwide-employees-engaged-work.aspx

23 Oswald, A. J., Proto, E., & Sgroi, D. (2015, October). Happiness and productivity. *Journal of Labor Economics, 33*(4), 789–822. https://doi.org/10.1086/681096

24 Martin, Judy. (n.d.) "Stress at Work Is Bunk for Business." *Forbes.* https://www.forbes.com/sites/work-in-progress/2012/08/02/stress-at-work-is-bunk-for-business/?sh=2108af5b5f89

25 *Sunday scaries: Exploring Sunday anxiety in America.* (2021, December 22). The Sleep Judge. https://www.thesleepjudge.com/sunday-scaries/

26 Mazur, C. (2022, January 23). *40+ worrisome workplace stress statistics [2022]: Facts, causes, and trends.* Zippia. https://www.stress.org/workplace-stress; Gallup. (2017). *State of the American workplace.* https://www.gallup.com/workplace/285818/state-american-workplace-report.aspx

27   Goh, J., Pfeffer, J., & Zenios, S. A. (2016, February). The relationship between workplace stressors and mortality and health costs in the United States. *Management Science*, 62(2), 608–628. https://doi.org/10.1287/mnsc.2014.2115

28   "Counting the cost of failure in drug development." 2017. Pharmaceutical Technology. June 19, 2017. https://www.pharmaceutical-technology.com/analysis/featurecounting-the-cost-of-failure-in-drug-development-5813046/.

29   Lo, B., & Field, M. J. (Eds.). (2009). *Conflict of interest in medical research, education, and practice*. Washington, DC: National Academies Press.

30   Lo, C. (2021, September 30). *Counting the cost of failure in drug development*. Pharmaceutical Technology https://www.pharmaceutical-technology.com/features/featurecounting-the-cost-of-failure-in-drug-development-5813046/

31   Schwartz, J., Bohdal-Spiegelhoff, U., Gretczko, M., & Sloan, N. (2016). *Global human capital trends 2016: The new organization: Different by design*. Deloitte University Press. https://www2.deloitte.com/content/dam/Deloitte/global/Documents/HumanCapital/gx-dup-global-human-capital-trends-2016.pdf

32   Stolp, S., & Smith, S. (1994). *School culture and climate: The role of the leader*. Eugene: Oregon School Study Council.

33   Schein, E. (2010). *The Handbook of Organizational Culture and Climate: Second ed.*

Chapter 2:
We All Resist Change

34   *Understanding the stress response: Chronic activation of this survival mechanism impairs health*. (2020, July 6). Harvard Health Publishing. https://www.health.harvard.edu/staying-healthy/understanding-the-stress-response

35   Selye, H., & Selye, H. (1956). *The stress of life*. New York: McGraw-Hill.

36   Somerfield, M. R., & Mccrae, R. R. (2000). Stress and coping research: Methodological challenges, theoretical advances, and clinical applications. *American Psychologist*, 55(6), 620–625. doi:10.1037/0003-066x.55.6.620

37   Stephens, M. A., & Wand, G. (2012). Stress and the HPA axis: Role of glucocorticoids in alcohol dependence. *Alcohol Research: Current Reviews*, 34(4), 468–483.

38   Reddy, M. S. (2017, August). Chronic stress: An etiological agent for the genesis of multitude of diseases, and the effect of meditation on modulating the stress. *Open Access Journal of Toxicology*, 1(5). https://doi.org/10.19080/oajt.2017.01.555571

39   van der Valk, E. S., Savas, M., & van Rossum, E. F. C. (2018). Stress and obesity: Are there more susceptible individuals? *Current Obesity Reports*, 7(2), 193–203. https://doi.org/10.1007/s13679-018-0306-y

40   Segerstrom, S. C., & Miller, G. E. (2004). Psychological stress and the human immune system: A meta-analytic study of 30 years of inquiry. *Psychological Bulletin*, 130(4), 601–630. https://doi.org/10.1037/0033-2909.130.4.601

41   Harbuz, M. S., Chover-Gonzalez, A. J., & Jessop, D. S. (2003, May). Hypothalamo-pituitary-adrenal axis and chronic immune activation. *Annals of the New York Academy of Sciences*, 992(1), 99–106. https://doi.org/10.1111/j.1749-6632.2003.tb03141.x

42   Yaribeygi, H., Panahi, Y., Sahraei, H., Johnston, T. P., & Sahebkar, A. (2017). The impact of stress on body function: A review. *EXCLI Journal*, 16, 1057–1072. https://doi.org/10.17179/excli2017-480

43   Marin, M., Lord, C., Andrews, J., Juster, R., Sindi, S., Arsenault-Lapierre, G., Fiocco, A. J., & Lupien, S. J. (2011, November). Chronic stress, cognitive functioning and mental health. *Neurobiology of Learning and Memory*, 96(4), 583–595. https://doi.org/10.1016/j.nlm.2011.02.016

44   Maier, S. F., & Seligman, M. E. (1976). Learned helplessness: Theory and evidence. *Journal of Experimental Psychology: General*, 105(1), 3–46. https://doi.org/10.1037/0096-3445.105.1.3

45   Selye, H. (1956). *The stress of life*. New York: McGraw-Hill.

46   World Health Organization. (2022, February). QD85 burnout. In *ICD-11 international classification of diseases* (11th ed.). https://icd.who.int/browse11/l-m/en#/http://id.who.int/icd/entity/129180281

47   Marmot, M. G., Bosma, H., Hemingway, H., Brunner, E., & Stansfeld, S. (1997, July 26). Contribution of job control and other risk factors to social variations in coronary heart disease incidence. *The Lancet*, 350(9073), 235–239. https://doi.org/10.1016/s0140-6736(97)04244-x; *Protect your brain from stress*. (2021, February 15). Harvard Health Publishing. https://www.health.harvard.edu/mind-and-mood/protect-your-brain-from-stress

48   Cooper, C. L., & Dewe, P. (2008, December). Well-being: Absenteeism, presenteeism, costs and challenges. *Occupational Medicine*, 58(8), 522–524. https://doi.org/10.1093/occmed/kqn124

49   McEwen, B. S., & Sapolsky, R. M. (1995, April). Stress and cognitive function. *Current Opinion in Neurobiology*, 5(2), 205–216. https://doi.org/10.1016/0959-4388(95)80028-x

50   Zhang, X., Ge, T. T., Yin, G., Cui, R., Zhao, G., & Yang, W. (2018). Stress-induced functional alterations in amygdala: Implications for neuropsychiatric diseases. *Frontiers in Neuroscience*, 12, 367. https://doi.org/10.3389/fnins.2018.00367

51   Lupien, S. J., Leon, M. D., de Santi, S., Convit, A., Tarshish, C., Nair, N. P. V., Thakur, M., McEwen, B. S., Hauger, R. L., & Meaney, M. J. (1998). Cortisol levels during human aging predict hippocampal atrophy and memory deficits. *Nature Neuroscience*, 1(1), 69–73. https://doi.org/10.1038/271

52   Dias-Ferreira, E., Sousa, J. C., Melo, I., Morgado, P., Mesquita, A. R., Cerqueira, J. J., Costa, R. M., & Sousa, N. (2009). Chronic stress causes frontostriatal reorganization and affects decision-making. *Science*, 325(5940), 621–625. https://doi.org/10.1126/science.1171203

53   Morgado, P., & Cerqueira, J. J. (2018). Editorial: The impact of stress on cognition and motivation. *Frontiers in Behavioral Neuroscience*, 12, 326. Https://doi.org/10.3389/fnbeh.2018.00326; Morgado, P., Marques, F., Ribeiro, B., Leite-Almeida, H., Pêgo, J. M., Rodrigues, A. J., Dalla, C., Kokras, N., Sousa, N., & Cerqueira, J. J. (2015, October). Stress induced risk-aversion is reverted by D2/D3 agonist in the rat. *European Neuropsychopharmacology*, 25(10), 1744–1752. https://doi.org/10.1016/j.euroneuro.2015.07.003; Sousa, N. (2016). The dynamics of the stress neuromatrix. *Molecular Psychiatry*, 21(3), 302–312. https://doi.org/10.1038/mp.2015.196

54   Kaplan, J. T., Gimbel, S. I., & Harris, S. (2016). Neural correlates of maintaining one's political beliefs in the face of counterevidence. *Scientific Reports*, 6(1). doi:10.1038/srep39589

55   Wilson, R. S., Arnold, S. E., Schneider, J. A., Li, Y., & Bennett, D. A. (2007). Chronic distress, age-related neuropathology, and late-life dementia. *Psychosomatic Medicine*, 69(1), 47–53. doi:10.1097/01.psy.0000250264.25017.21

56   Potts, H. (2019, September 30). A brain-changer: How stress redesigns our decision-making mind. Retrieved from https://thedecisionlab.com/insights/health/stress-redesigns-decision-making/

57   Scott, S. B., Graham-Engeland, J. E., Engeland, C. G., Smyth, J. M., Almeida, D. M., Katz, M. J., Lipton, R. B., Mogle, J. A., Munoz, E., Ram, N., & Sliwinski, M. J. (2015). The Effects of Stress on Cognitive Aging, Physiology and Emotion (ESCAPE) project. *BMC Psychiatry*, 15, 146. https://doi.org/10.1186/s12888-015-0497-7

58   Felps, W., Mitchell, T. R., & Byington, E. (2006). How, when, and why bad apples spoil the barrel: Negative group members and dysfunctional groups. *Research in Organizational Behavior*, 27, 175–222. doi:10.1016/s0191-3085(06)27005-9

59   *The future of jobs employment, skills and workforce strategy for the fourth industrial revolution.* (2016). World Economic Forum. doi:http://reports.weforum.org/future-of-jobs-2016/

Chapter 3:
The Power of Social Groups

60   Dunbar, R. I. (1998). The social brain hypothesis. *Evolutionary Anthropology: Issues, News, and Reviews*, 6(5), 178–190. doi:10.1002/(sici)1520-6505(1998)6:53.0.co;2-8

61   O'Donnell, M. B., Falk, E. B., & Lieberman, M. D. (2015). Social in, social out: How the brain responds to social language with more social language. *Communication Monographs*, 82(1), 31–63. doi:10.1080/03637751.2014.990472

62   Lieberman, M. D. (2015). *Social: Why our brains are wired to connect.* Oxford: Oxford University Press.

63   Bastardoz, N., & van Vugt, M. (2019). The nature of followership: Evolutionary analysis and review. *The Leadership Quarterly*, 30(1), 81–95. doi:10.1016/j.leaqua.2018.09.004

64   Eisenberger, N. I., Lieberman, M. D., & Williams, K. D. (2003). Does rejection hurt? An fMRI study of social exclusion. *Science*, 302(5643), 290–292. doi:10.1126/science.1089134

65   Eisenberger, N. I. (2012). The neural bases of social pain. *Psychosomatic Medicine*, 74(2), 126–135. doi:10.1097/psy.0b013e3182464dd1

66   Bruneau, E. G., Pluta, A., & Saxe, R. (2012). Distinct roles of the "shared pain" and 'theory of mind' networks in processing others' emotional suffering. *Neuropsychologia*, 50(2), 219–231. doi:10.1016/j.neuropsychologia.2011.11.008

67   Nagy, E., Pilling, K., Watt, R., Pal, A., & Orvos, H. (2017). Neonates' responses to repeated exposure to a still face. *Plos One*, 12(8). doi:10.1371/journal.pone.0181688; Bertin, E., & Striano, T. (2006). The still-face response in newborn, 1.5-, and 3-month-old infants. *Infant Behavior and Development*, 29(2), 294–297. doi:10.1016/j.infbeh.2005.12.003; Hsu, H., & Jeng, S. (2008). Two-month-olds' attention and affective response to maternal still face: A comparison between term and preterm infants in Taiwan. *Infant Behavior and Development*, 31(2), 194–206. doi:10.1016/j.infbeh.2007.10.008

68   Crabbe, R., Pivnick, L. K., Bates, J., Gordon, R. A., & Crosnoe, R. (2018). Contemporary college students' reflections on their high school peer crowds. *Journal of Adolescent Research*, 34(5), 563–596. doi:10.1177/0743558418809537

69   Bhanji, J. P., & Delgado, M. R. (2013). The social brain and reward: Social information processing in the human striatum. *Wiley Interdisciplinary Reviews: Cognitive Science*, 5(1), 61–73. doi:10.1002/wcs.1266

70   Lieberman, M. D., & Eisenberger, N. I. (2009). Neuroscience: Pains and pleasures of social life. *Science*, 323(5916), 890–891. doi:10.1126/science.1170008

71   Silk, J. B., & House, B. R. (2016). The evolution of altruistic social preferences in human groups. *Philosophical Transactions of the Royal Society B: Biological Sciences*, 371(1687), 20150097. doi:10.1098/rstb.2015.0097

72   Tabibnia, G., & Lieberman, M. D. (2007). Fairness and cooperation are rewarding: Evidence from social cognitive neuroscience. *Annals of the New York Academy of Sciences*, 1118(1), 90–101. doi:10.1196/annals.1412.001

73   England, P., Budig, M., & Folbre, N. (2002). Wages of virtue: The relative pay of care work. *Social Problems*, 49(4), 455–473. doi:10.1525/sp.2002.49.4.455

74   Bovey, W. H., & Hede, A. (2001). Resistance to organizational change: The role of cognitive and affective processes. *Leadership & Organization Development Journal*, 22(8), 372–382. doi:10.1108/01437730110410099

75   Jun, J. S. (2005). The self in the social construction of organizational reality: Eastern and Western views. *Administrative Theory & Praxis*, 27(1), 86–110. doi:10.1080/10841806.2005.11029475

76   Meyer, M. L., & Lieberman, M. D. (2018). Why people are always thinking about themselves: Medial prefrontal cortex activity during rest primes self-referential processing. *Journal of Cognitive Neuroscience*, 30(5), 714–721. doi:10.1162/jocn_a_01232

77   Mitchell, J. P., Macrae, C. N., & Banaji, M. R. (2006). Dissociable medial prefrontal contributions to judgments of similar and dissimilar others. *Neuron*, 50(4), 655–663. doi:10.1016/j.neuron.2006.03.040

78   Asch, S. E. (1955). Opinions and social pressure. *Scientific American*, 193(5), 31–35. doi:10.1038/scientificamerican1155-31; Asch, S. E. (1952). *Social psychology*. Englewood Cliffs, NJ: Prentice-Hall; Funt, A. (Writer). (1962). Face the rear [Television series episode]. In *Candid Camera*. CBS.

79   Vien, C. L. (2016, October 17). How groupthink can damage your organization: Welcoming differences of opinion leads to stronger decision-making. *CPA Insider*. https://www.journalofaccountancy.com/newsletters/2016/oct/groupthink-damage-organization.html

80   Van Vugt, M. V., Hogan, R., & Kaiser, R. B. (2008). Leadership, followership, and evolution: Some lessons from the past. *American Psychologist*, 63(3), 182–196. https://doi.org/10.1037/0003-066x.63.3.182; Kaplan, H., Hill, K., Lancaster, J., & Hurtado, A. M. (2000). A theory of human life history evolution: Diet, intelligence, and longevity. *Evolutionary Anthropology: Issues, News, and Reviews*, 9(4), 156–185. https://doi.org/10.1002/1520-6505(2000)9:4<156::AID-EVAN5>3.0.CO;2-7; Shamir, B. (2007). From passive recipients to active co-producers: The roles of followers in the leadership process. In B. Shamir, R. Pillai, M. C. Bligh, & M. Uhl-Bien (Eds.), *Follower-centered perspectives on leadership* (pp. ix–xxxix). Charlotte, NC: Information Age Publishing; Price, M. E., &

van Vugt, M. (2014). The evolution of leader-follower reciprocity: The theory of service-for-prestige. *Frontiers in Human Neuroscience*, 8(363), 1–17. https://doi.org/10.3389/fnhum.2014.00363

81 von Rueden, C., & van Vugt, M. (2015, December). Leadership in small-scale societies: Some implications for theory, research, and practice. *The Leadership Quarterly*, 26(6), 978–990. https://doi.org/10.1016/j.leaqua.2015.10.004

82 Smith, J. E., Gavrilets, S., Mulder, M. B., Hooper, P. L., Mouden, C. E., Nettle, D., Hauert, C., Perry, S., Pusey, A. E., & Smith, E. A. (2016). Leadership in mammalian societies: Emergence, distribution, power, and payoff. *Trends in Ecology & Evolution*, 31(1), 54–66. doi:10.1016/j.tree.2015.09.013

83 Vugt, M. V., & Ahuja, A. (2011). *Naturally selected: The evolutionary science of leadership*. New York: HarperBusiness.

84 Buss, D. M. (2016). *The handbook of evolutionary psychology*. Hoboken, NJ: Wiley.

85 Schaik, C. V. (2016). *The primate origins of human nature*. Hoboken: Wiley.

86 Longrich, N. (2020, September 27). What evolved faster—human brain or human society? Retrieved from https://scroll.in/article/972985/what-evolved-faster-human-brain-or-human-society#:~:text=So%20our%20societies%20and%20world,but%20by%20changing%20our%20cultures

87 van Vugt, M. (2006). Evolutionary origins of leadership and followership. *Personality and Social Psychology Review*, 10(4), 354–371. https://doi.org/10.1207/s15327957pspr1004_5

88 Henrich, J., & Gil-White, F. J. (2001). The evolution of prestige: Freely conferred deference as a mechanism for enhancing the benefits of cultural transmission. *Evolution and Human Behavior*, 22(3), 165–196. doi:10.1016/s1090-5138(00)00071-4; Maynard-Smith, J. (1982). *Evolution and the theory of games*. Cambridge: Cambridge University Press.

89 Sartori, R., Favretto, G., & Ceschi, A. (2013). The relationships between innovation and human and psychological capital in organizations: A review. *Innovation Journal*, 18, 1–18.

90 Schulze, A. D., Stade, M. J., & Netzel, J. (2014). Conflict and conflict management in innovation processes in the life sciences. *Creativity and Innovation Management*, 23(1), 57–75. doi:10.1111/caim.12048

91 Bolino, M., Long, D., & Turnley, W. (2016). Impression management in organizations: Critical questions, answers, and areas for future research. *Annual Review of Organizational Psychology and Organizational Behavior*, 3(1), 377–406. doi:10.1146/annurev-orgpsych-041015-062337

92 Nadella, S., Shaw, G., Nichols, J. T., & Gates, B. (2019). *Hit refresh: The quest to rediscover Microsoft's soul and imagine a better future for everyone*. New York: Harper Business.

93 Barabba, V. P. (2011). *The decision loom: A design for interactive decision-making in organizations*. Axminster, UK: Triarchy Press.

Chapter 4:
How Our Brains and Beliefs Limit Change

94 Center on the Developing Child. (2007). *The science of early childhood development*. InBrief, Harvard University. https://developingchild.harvard.edu/

95   Tseng, J., and Poppenk, J. (2020). Brain meta-state transitions demarcate thoughts across task contexts exposing the mental noise of trait neuroticism. *Nature Communications*, 11(1), 3480. https://doi.org/10.1038/s41467-020-17255-9

96   Connors, M. H., & Halligan, P. W. (2014). A cognitive account of belief: A tentative road map. *Frontiers in Psychology*, 5, 1588. https://doi.org/10.3389/fpsyg.2014.01588

97   Leahy, R. L. (1995, January). Cognitive development and cognitive therapy. *Journal of Cognitive Psychotherapy*, 9(3), 173–184. https://doi.org/10.1891/0889-8391.9.3.173

98   Bargh, J. A., & Morsella, E. (2008). The unconscious mind. *Perspectives on Psychological Science*, 3(1), 73–79. https://doi.org/10.1111/j.1745-6916.2008.00064.x

99   Ayan, S. (2018, December 19). The brain's autopilot mechanism steers consciousness. *Scientific American*. https://www.scientificamerican.com/article/the-brains-autopilot-mechanism-steers-consciousness/

100   Liberman, Z., Woodward, A. L., & Kinzler, K. D. (2017). The origins of social categorization. *Trends in Cognitive Sciences*, 21(7), 556–568. https://doi.org/10.1016/j.tics.2017.04.004

101   Halligan, P. W. (2006). Beliefs: Shaping experience and understanding illness. In P. Halligan & M. Aylward (Eds.), *The power of belief: Psychosocial influence on illness, disability, and medicine* (pp. xi–xxvi). Oxford: Oxford University Press. https://doi.org/10.1093/med:psych/9780198530114.001.0001

102   The Urban Child Institute (n.d.). *Baby's brain begins now: Conception to age 3*. Retrieved August 26, 2022, from http://www.urbanchildinstitute.org/why-0-3/baby-and-brain

103   Festinger, L., Riecken, H. W., & Schachter, S. (1956). *When prophecy fails: A social and psychological study of a modern group that predicted the destruction of the world*. Minneapolis: University of Minnesota Press.

104   Steele, C. M., & Aronson, J. (1995). Stereotype threat and the intellectual test performance of African Americans. *Journal of Personality and Social Psychology*, 69(5), 797–811. doi:10.1037/0022-3514.69.5.797

105   Steele, C. M., & Aronson, J. (1995). Stereotype threat and the intellectual test performance of African Americans. *Journal of Personality and Social Psychology*, 69(5), 797–811. doi:10.1037/0022-3514.69.5.797

106   Hood, B. M. (2013). The self illusion: How the social brain creates identity. Toronto: HarperCollins Canada.

107   Maslow, A. H. (1943). A theory of human motivation. *Psychological Review*, 50(4), 370–396. https://doi.org/10.1037/h0054346

Chapter 5:
What to Expect on the Journey Ahead

108   Darwin, C. (1873). *On the origin of species by means of natural selection, or the preservation of favoured races in the struggle for life* (6th ed., p. 85). London: John Murray.

109   Bourke, A. F. (2011). Expanded view of social evolution. In *Principles of social evolution*. Oxford: Oxford University Press. doi:10.1093/acprof:oso/9780199231157.003.0001

110   Kolb, B., & Whishaw, I. Q. (2009). *Fundamentals of human neuropsychology* (pp. 718–735). New York: Worth Publishers.

111   Schwartz, J. M., & Begley, S. (2002). *The mind and the brain: Neuroplasticity and the power of mental force* (p. 236). New York: Regan Books.

112   Rock, D., & Schwartz, J., (2006, Summer). The neuroscience of leadership. *Strategy+Business* 43. https://www.strategy-business.com/article/06207

Chapter 6:
A Unique Adventure

113   van Vugt, M., Hogan, R., & Kaiser, R. B. (2008). Leadership, followership, and evolution: Some lessons from the past. *American Psychologist*, 63(3), 182–196. https://doi.org/10.1037/0003-066x.63.3.182

114   Daisyme, P. (2015, August 12). The unique cultures of 10 hugely successful companies. *Entrepreneur*. https://www.entrepreneur.com/article/249293

115   Taylor, B. (2019, December 16). To build a strong culture, create rules that are unique to your company. *Harvard Business Review*. https://hbr.org/2019/12/to-build-a-strong-culture-create-rules-that-are-unique-to-your-company

116   Daisyme, P. (2015, August 12). The unique cultures of 10 hugely successful companies. *Entrepreneur*. https://www.entrepreneur.com/article/249293

117   Ramaswamy, V., & Banta, K. (2017, March 14). This pharma company stays innovative by doing two things. *Harvard Business Review*. https://hbr.org/2017/03/this-pharma-company-stays-innovative-by-doing-two-things

118   Horowitz, B. (2019). *What you do is who you are: How to create your business culture*. New York: Harper Business.

119   Taylor, B. (2019, December 3). To build a strong culture, create rules that are unique to your company. *Harvard Business Review*. https://hbr.org/2019/12/to-build-a-strong-culture-create-rules-that-are-unique-to-your-company

Chapter 7:
Envisioning a New Environment

120   Webster-Stratton, C. (2006). *How to promote children's social and emotional competence*. London: Paul Chapman Publishing.

121   Edmondson, A. C. (1996, March). Learning from mistakes is easier said than done: Group and organizational influences on the detection and correction of human error. *The Journal of Applied Behavioral Science*, 32(1), 5–28. https://doi.org/10.1177/0021886396321001

122   Duhigg, C. (2016, February 28). What Google learned from its quest to build the perfect team. *The New York Times*. https://www.nytimes.com/2016/02/28/magazine/what-google-learned-from-its-quest-to-build-the-perfect-team.html

123   Rozovsky, J. (2015, November 17). *The five keys to a successful Google team*. reWork. https://rework.withgoogle.com/blog/five-keys-to-a-successful-google-team/

124 Edmondson, A. (1999). Psychological safety and learning behavior in work teams. *Administrative Science Quarterly*, 44(2), 350–383. https://doi.org/10.2307/2666999; Kahn, W. A. (1990). Psychological conditions of personal engagement and disengagement at work. *Academy of Management Journal*, 33(4), 692–724. https://doi.org/10.5465/256287

125 Duhigg, C. (2016, February 28). What Google learned from its quest to build the perfect team. *The New York Times*. https://www.nytimes.com/2016/02/28/magazine/what-google-learned-from-its-quest-to-build-the-perfect-team.html

126 Edmondson, A. C. (2004). Psychological safety, trust, and learning in organizations: A group-level lens. In R. M. Kramer & K. S. Cook (Eds.), *Trust and distrust in organizations: Dilemmas and approaches* (pp. 239–272). New York: Russell Sage Foundation.

127 Werner, E. E., & Smith, R. S. (1979, Spring). A report from the Kauai longitudinal study. *Journal of the American Academy of Child Psychiatry*, 18(2), 292–306. https://doi.org/10.1016/s0002-7138(09)61044-x

128 Masten, A. S. (2014). *Ordinary magic: Resilience in development*. New York: The Guilford Publications.

129 Luthar, S. S., & Eisenberg, N. (2017). Developmental research and translational science: Evidence-based interventions for at-risk youth and families child development. *Child Development*, 88(2), 337–349. https://doi.org/10.1111/cdev.12737; Troy, A. S., & Mauss, I. B. (2011). Resilience in the face of stress: Emotion regulation as a protective factor. In S. M. Southwick, B. T. Litz, D. Charney, & M. J. Friedman (Eds.), *Resilience and mental health: Challenges across the lifespan* (pp. 30–44). Cambridge: Cambridge University Press.

130 Hartwig, A., Clarke, S., Johnson, S., & Willis, S. (2020). Workplace team resilience: A systematic review and conceptual development. *Organizational Psychology Review*, 10(3–4), 169–200. https://doi.org/10.1177/2041386620919476

131 Gallup. (2015). *The state of the American manager: Analytics and advice for leaders*. https://www.aseonline.org/images/marketing/StateOfAmericanManager_Gallup.pdf

132 Mann, A., & McCarville, B. (2015, November 13). What job-hopping employees are looking for. *Gallup Business Journal*. https://news.gallup.com/businessjournal/186602/job-hopping-employees-looking.aspx

133 Vallerand, R. J., Paquet, Y., Philippe, F. L., & Charest, J. (2010, February). On the role of passion for work in burnout: A process model. *Journal of Personality*, 78(1), 289–312. https://doi.org/10.1111/j.1467-6494.2009.00616.x

134 Ballinger, G. A., Cross, R., & Holtom, B. C. (2016). The right friends in the right places: Understanding network structure as a predictor of voluntary turnover. *Journal of Applied Psychology*, 101(4), 535–548. https://doi.org/10.1037/apl0000061

135 Edmondson, A. C. (2019). *The fearless organization: Creating psychological safety in the workplace for learning, innovation, and growth* (pp. 17–19). Hoboken, NJ: Wiley.

136 Accountability. (n.d.). *Merriam-Webster.com dictionary*. Retrieved August 26, 2022, from https://www.merriam-webster.com/dictionary/accountability

137 Maslow, A. H. (1943). A theory of human motivation. *Psychological Review*, 50(4), 370–396. https://doi.org/10.1037/h0054346

Chapter 8:
Becoming a Trusted Leader—It Starts with You

138   Goleman, D. (2001). Neurological substrates of EI. In C. Cherniss & D. Goleman (Eds.), *The emotionally intelligent workplace: How to select for, measure, and improve emotional intelligence in individuals, groups, and organizations* (pp. 29–32). San Francisco: Jossey-Bass.

139   Beck, J. S. (2011). *Cognitive behavior therapy: Basics and beyond* (p. 35). New York: The Guilford Press.

140   Beck, A. T. (1963). Thinking and depression: I. Idiosyncratic content and cognitive distortions. *Archives of General Psychiatry*, 9(4), 324–333. https://doi.org/10.1001/archpsyc.1963.01720160014002

141   Fosnot, C. T. (Ed.). (1996). *Constructivism: Theory, perspectives, and practice* (p. ix). New York: Teachers College Press; Andrews, T. (2012, June). What is social constructionism? *Grounded Theory Review*, 11(1), 39–46. http://groundedtheoryreview.com/2012/06/01/what-is-social-constructionism/

142   Teasdale, J. D. (1983). Negative thinking in depression: Cause, effect, or reciprocal relationship? *Advances in Behaviour Research and Therapy*, 5(1), 3–25. https://doi.org/10.1016/0146-6402(83)90013-9

143   Plato. (2016). Apology (C. D. C. Reeve, Trans.). In S. M. Cohen, P. Curd, & C. D. C. Reeve (Eds.), *Readings in ancient Greek philosophy: From Thales to Aristotle* (5th ed., p. 104). Indianapolis: Hackett Publishing Company.

144   Lipman, Victor (n.d.). All successful leaders need this quality: Self-awareness. *Forbes*. https://www.forbes.com/sites/victorlipman/2013/11/18/all-successful-leaders-need-this-quality-self-awareness/?sh=3e4555311f06

145   Avolio, B. J., & Gardner, W. L. (2005, June). Authentic leadership development: Getting to the root of positive forms of leadership. *The Leadership Quarterly*, 16(3), 315–338. https://doi.org/10.1016/j.leaqua.2005.03.001

146   McAdams, D. P. (1997). *The stories we live by: Personal myths and the making of the self* (pp. 269–277). New York: The Guilford Press.

147   Hougaard, R., Carter, J., & Brewerton, V. (2018, January 29). Why do so many managers forget they're human beings? *Harvard Business Review*. https://hbr.org/2018/01/why-do-so-many-managers-forget-theyre-human-beings

148   Carden, J., Jones, R. J., & Passmore, J. (2022). Defining self-awareness in the context of adult development: A systematic literature review. *Journal of Management Education*, 46(1), 1–38. https://doi.org/10.1177/1052562921990065

149   Brown, B. (2010). *The gifts of imperfection: Let go of who you think you're supposed to be and embrace who you are*. City Center, MN: Hazelden.

150   Brown, B. (2018). *Dare to lead* (p. 126). New York: Random House.

151   Brown, B. (2006). Shame resilience theory: A grounded theory study on women and shame. *Families in Society: The Journal of Contemporary Social Services*, 87(1), 43–52. https://doi.org/10.1606/1044-3894.3483

152 Ilies, R., Morgeson, F. P., & Nahrgang, J. D. (2005, June). Authentic leadership and eudaemonic well-being: Understanding leader-follower outcomes. *The Leadership Quarterly*, 16(3), 373–394. https://doi.org/10.1016/j.leaqua.2005.03.002

153 Gardner, W. L., Avolio, B. J., Luthans, F., May, D. R., & Walumbwa, F. (2005, June). "Can you see the real me?" A self-based model of authentic leader and follower development. *The Leadership Quarterly*, 16(3), 343–372. https://doi.org/10.1016/j.leaqua.2005.03.003

154 Clifton, J. (2017, April 27). *Are you sure you have a great workplace culture?* Gallup Workplace. https://www.gallup.com/workplace/251642/manager.aspx

Chapter 9:
Building a Leadership Team

155 Curnow-Chavez, A. (2018, April 10). 4 ways to deal with a toxic coworker. *Harvard Business Review*. https://hbr.org/2018/04/4-ways-to-deal-with-a-toxic-coworker

156 Groysberg, B., Polzer, J. T., & Elfenbein, H. A. (2011, May–June). Too many cooks spoil the broth: How high status individuals decrease group effectiveness. *Organization Science*, 22(3), 722–737. https://doi.org/10.1287/orsc.1100.0547

157 Grant, A. (2016). *Originals: How non-conformists move the world* (pp. 191–196). New York: Penguin Books.

158 Adams, L., Curnow-Chavez, A., Epstein, A., Teasdale, R., & Berger, J. (2017). *The loyalist team: How trust, candor, and authenticity create great organizations.* New York: PublicAffairs.

159 Lennick, D., & Kiel, F. (2007). Moral intelligence: Enhancing business performance and leadership success. Upper Saddle River, NJ: Wharton School Publishing.

160 Bennett, L. M., & Gadlin, H. (2012). Collaboration and team science: From theory to practice. *Journal of Investigative Medicine*, 60(5), 768–775. https://doi.org/10.2310/jim.0b013e318250871d

Chapter 10:
Setting the Scene for Engagement

161 Taylor, S. (2019). *The psychology of pandemics: Preparing for the next global outbreak of infectious disease.* Newcastle, UK: Cambridge Scholars Publishing.

162 Centola, D., Becker, J., Brackbill, D., & Baronchelli, A. (2018). Experimental evidence for tipping points in social convention. *Science*, 360(6393), 1116–1119. https://doi.org/10.1126/science.aas8827; Gladwell, M. (2015). *The tipping point: How little things can make a big difference.* London: Abacus.

163 Duan, L., Sheeren, E., & Weiss, L. M. (2014, March 1). Tapping the power of hidden influencers. *McKinsey Quarterly*. https://www.mckinsey.com/business-functions/people-and-organizational-performance/our-insights/tapping-the-power-of-hidden-influencers

164 Rogers, E. M. (1967). *Bibliography on the diffusion of innovations.* East Lansing, MI: Department of Communication, Michigan State University.

165   Kotter, J. P. (2012). *Leading change*. Boston: Harvard Business Review Press; Kotter, J. P., & Whitehead, L. A. (2010). *Buy in: Saving your good idea from getting shot down* (p. 183). Boston: Harvard Business Review Press; Bridges, W., & Mitchell, S. (2000). Leading transition: A new model for change. *Leader to Leader*, 16(3), 30–36.

166   Kolb, B., & Whishaw, I. Q. (2001). *An introduction to brain and behavior* (p. 542). New York: Worth Publishers.

167   Schacter, D. L., & Buckner, R. L. (1998). Priming and the brain. *Neuron*, 20(2), 185–195. https://doi.org/10.1016/S0896-6273(00)80448-1

168   Gallistel, C. R. (2001). Mental representations, psychology of. In N. J. Smelser & P. B. Baltes (Eds.), *International encyclopedia of the social and behavioral sciences* (pp. 9691–9695). New York: Elsevier. https://doi.org/10.1016/B0-08-043076-7/01488-1

169   Mack, M. L., Preston, A. R., & Love, B. C. (2013). Decoding the brain's algorithm for categorization from its neural implementation. *Current Biology*, 23(20), 2023–2027. https://doi.org/10.1016/j.cub.2013.08.035

170   Lant, J. L. (1987). *Money making marketing: Finding the people who need what you're selling and making sure they buy it*. Cambridge, MA: JLA Publications.

171   Nickerson, R. S. (1998). Confirmation bias: A ubiquitous phenomenon in many guises. *Review of General Psychology*, 2(2), 175–220. https://doi.org/10.1037/1089-2680.2.2.175; Anderson, C. A. (1982). Inoculation and counterexplanation: Debiasing techniques in the perseverance of social theories. *Social Cognition*, 1(2), 126–139. doi:10.1521/soco.1982.1.2.126

Chapter 11:
Understanding the Current State

172   "L&D in M&A: It starts with an honest culture assessment." (n.d.) HR Dive. https://www.hrdrive.com/news/id-in-ma-it-starts-with-an-honest-culture-assessment/572927/

173   Hinton, P. (2017). Implicit stereotypes and the predictive brain: Cognition and culture in "biased" person perception. *Palgrave Communications*, 3(1), 17086. https://doi.org/10.1057/palcomms.2017.86

174   Kraut, A. I. (Ed.). (1996). *Organizational surveys: Tools for assessment and change*. San Francisco: Pfeiffer.

175   Baruch, Y., & Holtom, B. C. (2008). Survey response rate levels and trends in organizational research. *Human Relations*, 61(8), 1139–1160. https://doi.org/10.1177/0018726708094863

176   Lindemann, N. (2021, August 9). *What's the average survey response rate?* PointerPro. https://surveyanyplace.com/average-survey-response-rate/

177   Morrel-Samuels, P. (2002, February). Getting the truth into workplace surveys. *Harvard Business Review*. https://hbr.org/2002/02/getting-the-truth-into-workplace-surveys

178   Bruneau, E. G., & Saxe, R. (2012, July). The power of being heard: The benefits of "perspective-giving" in the context of intergroup conflict. *Journal of Experimental Social Psychology*, 48(4), 855–866. https://doi.org/10.1016/j.jesp.2012.02.017

179 Bohart, A. C. (1991). Empathy in client-centered therapy: A contrast with psychoanalysis and self psychology. *Journal of Humanistic Psychology*, 31(1), 34–48. https://doi.org/10.1177/0022167891311003

180 Weger, H., Castle Bell, G., Minei, E. M., & Robinson, M. C. (2014). The relative effectiveness of active listening in initial interactions. *International Journal of Listening*, 28(1), 13–31. https://doi.org/10.1080/10904018.2013.813234

Chapter 12:
A Scientific Experiment

181 Megginson, L. C. (1963, June). Lessons from Europe for American business. *Southwestern Social Science Quarterly*, 44(1), 3–13. https://www.jstor.org/stable/42866937

182 Freud, S. (1958). The dynamics of transference. In J. Strachey (Ed.), *The standard edition of the complete psychological works of Sigmund Freud, volume XII (1911–1913): The case of Schreber, papers on technique and other works* (pp. ii–vii). London: The Hogarth Press and the Institute of Psycho-analysis.

183 Edmondson, A. C. (2013). *Teaming to innovate* (p. 48). San Francisco: Jossey-Bass.

184 Carleton, R. N. (2016). Fear of the unknown: One fear to rule them all? *Journal of Anxiety Disorders*, 41, 5–21. https://doi.org/10.1016/j.janxdis.2016.03.011

185 Steijaert, M. J., Schaap, G., & Van't Riet, J. (2020). Two-sided science: Communicating scientific uncertainty increases trust in scientists and donation intention by decreasing attribution of communicator bias. *Communications*, 46(2). https://doi.org/10.1515/commun-2019-0123; Allen, J., Jimmieson, N. L., Bordia, P., & Irmer, B. E. (2007). Uncertainty during organizational change: Managing perceptions through communication. *Journal of Change Management*, 7(2), 187–210. https://doi.org/10.1080/14697010701563379

186 Glassdoor. (2019). *Mission & culture survey 2019*. https://about-content.glassdoor.com//app/uploads/sites/2/2019/07/Mission-Culture-Survey-Supplement.pdf; Society for Human Resource Management (SHRM). (2016). *Employee job satisfaction and engagement: Revitalizing a changing workforce*. https://www.shrm.org/hr-today/trends-and-forecasting/research-and-surveys/Documents/2016-Employee-Job-Satisfaction-and-Engagement-Report.pdf

Made in the USA
Columbia, SC
13 December 2022

73801487R00152